REA

9 MYTHS THAT DAMAGE
A CHILD'S CONFIDENCE

"**CONFIDENCE** is when you can face your worst nightmares."—Fourth grader

"**CONFIDENCE** is when children tell their parents what they feel inside without being scared."—Third grader

"**CONFIDENCE** is when I want to do something hard, and inside something is encouraging me to do it."—Third grader

"**CONFIDENCE** is when you need to do a scary thing and you are not afraid to do it."—Third grader

"**CONFIDENCE** is something a person has so that he can complete something he has to do."—Fifth grader

"**CONFIDENCE** is trusting God to do something or prevent something as well as believing in God to help you do something accurately."—Third grader

9 Myths That Damage a Child's Confidence

What Parents Think, What Children Say, What Professionals Observe

Pat Holt

Harold Shaw Publishers
Wheaton, Illinois

The author has made every effort to trace sources of quotes. Where acknowledgment is inadvertently omitted, the author expresses her regret.

Scripture quotations marked NASB are taken from the New American Standard Bible, © 1960, 1962, 1963, 1968, 1971, 1972, 1973, 1975, 1977 by The Lockman Foundation. Used by permission.

Scripture quotations marked NIV are taken from the HOLY BIBLE, NEW INTERNATIONAL VERSION®. NIV®. Copyright © 1973, 1978, 1984 International Bible Society. Used by permission of Zondervan Publishing House. All rights reserved.

The "NIV" and "New International Version" trademarks are registered in the United States Patent and Trademark Office by International Bible Society. Use of either trademark requires permission of International Bible Society.

Scripture quotations marked NKJV are taken from The New King James Version. Copyright © 1979, 1980, 1982, Thomas Nelson Inc., Publishers.

Scripture quotations marked TLB are taken from *The Living Bible* © 1971. Used by permission of Tyndale House Publishers, Inc., Wheaton IL 60189. All rights reserved.

ISBN 0-87788-591-5

Cover design by David LaPlaca
Cover photo © 1999 by F. Franke/SuperStock

Library of Congress Cataloging-in-Publication Data

Holt, Pat. 1943–
    9 myths that damage a child's confidence / Pat Holt.
        p.   cm.
    ISBN 0-87788-591-5 (pbk.)
    1. Family—Religious life. 2. Child rearing—Religious aspects—
Christianity. 3. Confidence in children—Religious aspects—
Christianity. I. Title. II. Title: Nine myths that damage a child's
confidence.
BV4526.2.H63 1999   99-24186
248.8'45–dc21   CIP

03 02 01 00 99
8 7 6 5 4 3 2 1

With love and gratitude to my
confidence-building family—Mom, Dad,
my beloved and God-confident Dave,
and my wonderful God-confident children,
Gary, Candice, and Andrew

For all the precious children and parents
who shared their thoughts and feelings
with such honesty and candor

Contents

Preface

A confident person is a courageous person, a person who can face the inevitable risks and challenges of life without crippling fear.

A confident child will not be crushed when someone calls him a name, when she is not chosen for the team, or when he is not invited to the party. A confident child will not be afraid to try something new.

A confident parent does not insist on unreasonable control of the child or feel obligated to manipulate situations involving the child. A confident parent will not crumble when faced with the inevitable discovery that life is not fair for the beloved child.

What is the source of confidence? In what can we be confident? Throughout history, most people would have answered, "in God" (or "the gods"). Since the rise of humanism, the usual modern answer is, "In ourselves and our own abilities." In recent decades, self-confidence has been touted as a sure way to success.

SELF-confidence looks inside and feels totally capable of meeting the challenges of life, alone and unaided. SELF-confidence insists, "I can do it." "I am the master of my fate, I am the captain of my soul." While this rhetoric sounds heady and exciting, it simply isn't true—no human controls his or her own destiny.

GOD-confidence looks to God as the loving sovereign, in control of all things everywhere at all times. Because of this, God is worthy of trust without reservation. GOD-confidence says, "I will trust in the Lord with all my heart. I will not lean on my own understanding. In all my ways I will acknowledge the Lord, and he will make my paths straight" (Proverbs 3:5-6, paraphrased).

God-confident parents are able to trust the Lord to be in control of each situation involving their child even when the outcome is contrary to their desires or expectations. A God-confident parent does not worry excessively or endlessly attempt to control everything.

A God-confident child will grow up in accordance with Daniel 11:32, "But the people who know their God will display strength and take action" (NASB). He or she trusts in God and the abilities that God has given.

It is my earnest desire and fervent prayer that this book will help and encourage you to raise children who have this God-confidence.

Acknowledgments

A book is a team effort. This little book could not have been conceived or written without the ongoing help and cooperation of the "Confidence Team." Many thanks to the entire team!

Joan Guest, editorial director, came up with the idea for the book and gave helpful, friendly advice along the way.

Joyce Farrell, my friend and agent, has been an unfailing source of encouragement through our years together.

Shirle and Dan Luttio are dear friends who encouraged me with kind words and beautiful flowers.

Trudi Ponder is my cherished prayer partner. She listens and knows how to pray.

Liz George, my precious friend and fellow writer, does not cease to pray and to care.

The Bickdrews—Larry, Victoria, Debbie, and John—are much loved long-time friends who thought, prayed, and shared. Victoria jogged my memory to remind me of appropriate stories.

Patty Mac and Lorrie Marahunich, two treasured friends and coworkers for many years, reminded me of people, places, and things to share with readers.

Introduction

Dear Parents:

I well remember one warm day when the "weather" suddenly changed in my office. I could feel a chill as a thirty-something couple entered. The appointment was not their idea. It was scheduled by the school staff to deal with the growing academic and behavioral problems of their sixth grader. They stiffened as they listened to the teachers. Then they became defensive and blamed the school for the child's problems. The teachers and I listened patiently as we heard the familiar excuses.

We understood that the parents loved their child and would do anything for him. That was a given. Why else would they sacrifice to pay tuition for private schooling? We wanted to communicate in a gentle way that it was time for the child to take responsibility for the consequences of his actions.

We wanted to impress on the parents that continuing to rescue their child from the consequences of his poor choices would lead to an ever increasing lack of confidence, but that learning to accept responsibility for his actions would increase his confidence and improve his behavior.

The parents were fearful. The mother had been raised in an atmosphere of rigid, authoritarian, parental control. The father had no parental involvement, was left alone most of the time, allowed to go his own way and do his own thing. They were fearful of not showing the love, support, and loyalty they had so longed for and never received in their own childhoods.

As the conference went on, each parent softened,

realizing that our goals for their son were the same. Each of us wanted their son to develop into a man of strong character with the confidence to achieve and the confidence to make tough decisions and to stand alone when it was the right thing to do.

After a long time, the father's voice broke. "I wonder what I could have been if my parents had cared enough to be there for me and give me confidence. I wouldn't have wasted so many years getting involved with the things that have scarred my life and kept me from being the man I wanted to be."

The mother began to sob. "Even now I don't have any confidence. I'm easily intimidated. I don't want that to happen to my son."

In different ways with different children, that story has been repeated to me literally thousands of times over the past thirty years. I know that a heart's desire for the vast majority of parents is to raise confident children. They want their children to have more confidence than they had growing up.

No wonder! A truly confident person is optimistic, courageous, secure, hopeful, lighthearted, self-assured, self-sufficient, has strong belief with full assurance, is enthusiastic, positive, certain, and untroubled, having a state of mind free from doubt or misgivings.

The American writer Anne Morrow Lindbergh aptly described lack of confidence when she said, "The most exhausting thing in life is to be insecure." Because most of us know all too well the exhaustion that insecurity brings, we do not want that for our children.

Is it possible for parents to raise confident children even if their own childhoods did not model confidence building? Absolutely! From my experience, I have seen it happen over and over again as parents, children, and educators work together as a team to build a solid foundation of God-confidence in a child.

I love to talk with children and listen to them. In

preparation for writing this book, I asked 250 children between the ages of eight and thirteen to anonymously answer three questions in writing:

- What is confidence?

- What should a parent do to build a child's confidence? Give an example.

- What should a parent NOT do to build a child's confidence? Give an example.

With each age group, the answers were written with no discussion. I wanted to know what the children thought on their own, without being influenced by their peer group.

Their honesty and sincerity is heart warming and, at times, heart wrenching. Some of their answers are shared in this book so that we parents can fully understand not only how our children see us, but also how we can make necessary adjustments to build more confident children.

I also interviewed young and older adults, many of whom are parents. I asked three questions:

- What did your parents do that helped you to grow confident?

- What did your parents do that hindered your confidence?

- What will you do or not do (What are you doing or not doing) as a parent to raise confident children?

In addition to sharing some of their stories, further insight and understanding will be shared from interviews with professional educators and family counselors.

As you read, you may find yourself experiencing mixed emotions. Undoubtedly you will be positively affirmed in many things that you are doing to raise confident children. Perhaps you will also feel somewhat guilty as you identify some of the ways that children believe their confidence is being hindered. Then, too, you will be challenged to discover ways to adjust your parenting to encourage confidence in your children.

I urge you to take the three-step "Start-Stop-Continue Confidence Test" with each chapter, which consists of answering three questions:

→ What could you START doing to build your child's confidence?

→ What should you STOP doing in order to build your child's confidence?

→ What should you CONTINUE to do to raise confident children?

Asking these three questions can help you identify what works and what doesn't work to achieve your parenting goal of raising confident children.

I look forward to our journey together through this book—to make you the best parent you can be!

Pat Holt

1

"My Child Will Crumble If I Don't Stand Up for Him"

"Confidence is something that helps you stand your ground and know that you can do it."
—Third grader

"Confidence is standing up for what you believe in even if you're standing alone."
—Fourth grader

After weeks of eager anticipation, the track team uniforms came. School was over. The boys eagerly tried on the uniforms before practice. They were all quite large. The coach watched the boys proudly parade around in the uniforms, then turned and went to the equipment shed for something needed but forgotten.

During this brief period of time, one of the boys got the idea to pull someone's shorts down. It didn't take much effort, since some of them were so big they were nearly falling off anyway. Unfortunately, the hilarious reaction caused a number of such "pantsing" incidents within seconds.

One of the members of the team thought the whole thing was just too much fun and took the opportunity to "pants" a boy who had been his best friend through all of elementary school. There was great enjoyment and laughter on the part of both boys and the rest of the team. Needless to add, the boys were all wearing undershorts. The oblivious coach returned to a track team totally under control.

The school was unaware of the incident until three days later when the best friend told his teacher. The teacher and I spoke with each of the best friends separately, as well as with the other members of the track team. The stories corroborated the multiple incidents. Apologies and appropriate consequences followed as well as future warnings of more severe consequences if the "pantsing" were ever repeated. The parents of the boy who started it were extremely supportive of the school, and their impulsive son was also given consequences at home. Uniforms that were overly large were sent back to the company for smaller sizes as a sensible and precautionary measure to avoid such future temptations!

But all that was not nearly enough for the father of the "best friend." He came to school literally shaking with rage. He had contacted an attorney and was certain that his son was a victim of sexual harassment. He also believed that this was a plot by the other boys to humiliate his son, that others on the school campus had witnessed the degrading event, and that all were part of the plot. He was particularly angry with his son's friend.

After several painful days for the "best friend," his family, and the school, the father dropped his legal maneuvers, feeling that all the parties had shown that they took the matter seriously. The sad result, however, was that the best friends' relationship of many years was killed. The father did not even want his son speaking to the other boy. Before this incident, the boys had been almost inseparable.

When Parents Intervene

Many times, well-meaning parents overreact. Parental

overreacting can cause confidence problems for a child.

A fifth grader answered the question, "What should a parent NOT do to build a child's confidence?" with this telling statement: "Talking back to teachers and the principal is not good for a child's confidence."

In reality, this could have been written about any one of a number of well-meaning parents who love their children and who really believe Myth Number One: "My child will crumble if I don't stand up for him."

No educator or therapist is surprised by this child's assessment. Many of today's parents are as eager to show their love for their children by overreacting to everyday situations as yesterday's parents were resolved to build the character of their children by underreacting.

Who Did the Work?

In the fifth grade at our school, children are expected to do a state report. Because these reports involve displays for open house, supportive parents often become involved. Although limitations regarding the size and scope of the projects are clearly delineated in writing, the displays frequently become somewhat lavish and overdone, especially for an elementary school.

In preparation for this assignment, two families in our school each had a similar idea. They would gather material from the state that they visited during the summer and be way ahead when the assignment was given. What a great idea! Can't you just imagine the fun these families had in planning the report, taking pictures, gathering materials, and determining how each of the collected pieces would be displayed?

One small planning problem occurred for both families. Neither family had checked with their child's fifth-grade teacher to see if the state selected was going to be the state assigned.

The experienced and highly esteemed fifth-grade teacher had been allowing children to select their states the same way for the past thirteen years: To be fair, each child's name was put in a container. Several months after school was in session, the teacher would shake up the container in front of the class, draw a name, and the child chosen would then select a state. Since there were more states than children, each child in the class was required to select a different state.

At the beginning of the year, the parents and children in the fifth grade were informed as to the way the state for the report would be selected.

Unfortunately, by the "luck of the draw," neither child was able to select the state visited during the summer, the state for which all the time, planning, and emotional energy had been invested. Each of those states had already been chosen by children whose names were drawn earlier.

For one parent, the trauma was too great. The mother insisted that the child's present and future self-esteem was in danger and that it was imperative that the teacher make an exception for her child. The teacher patiently reiterated what she had said earlier in the year. This did not satisfy.

The distressed parent came to the office. I was not there. She said that I needed to be called at home that night because the matter was of such urgency and importance. The secretary listened with compassion, smiled with understanding, and put the message in my box, to be retrieved in the morning.

The situation had become increasingly emotional for the parent, who arrived at the school office the following morning, lugging two cumbersome and very heavy bags full of collected materials for me to see so that I would fully understand the situation.

I helped the concerned mother drag the bags into my office. I listened. My mother's heart understood the parent's plea. My administrator's head understood the teacher, who had done everything correctly. What to do? I asked God for wisdom, as the conference began.

I listened once again to the parent's logic as she described the potential devastation to her daughter unless the exception was made, and to the teacher's patient reiteration of the handling of the assignment, to which no parent had objected in thirteen years. I also kept looking at the bags of collected treasures now taking up considerable office space.

I loved the teacher and needed to support her. I had actually known the parent longer than the teacher and loved her also. Through the years, the mom had spent literally thousands of hours at school helping in a variety of ways.

Finally, I suggested that the child be required to do the assignment given, but that, if it were acceptable to the teacher, she could also have the opportunity to display the collectibles. The teacher agreed. The mom said she would see if her daughter would accept the compromise. She did.

What of the other family, whom I had also known for years, and who also love and support their child and want to do the best for their child?

That mother was able to shrug off the disappointment, letting her daughter know that sometimes God allows these kinds of things to happen, even though we don't like them and don't always understand. The mother assured the daughter that she would help her with the state assignment and that they would have a lot of fun learning about a new state they had not visited. The family decided that if they really enjoyed studying about the state, perhaps they would visit the following summer.

An insightful fifth grader wrote, "One thing a parent should not do to build a child's confidence is force it. Parents can help but they can't do it for you. A parent should listen to the child's feelings. They should *not* talk for the child."

Striking a Balance

The children are begging for parental balance. They want parents to listen, to understand, and to be on their side, but they don't want their parents to rob them of the opportunity to be themselves, to develop their confidence, and to grow strong by handling the inevitable storms and struggles of childhood.

When situations arise where you, the loving parent, are tempted to jump on your white horse of protection to shield and defend your child against the evils of injustice, take time to assess the situation. Should your role be as the parent who teaches a child how to handle the situation alone? Or is it necessary for you to champion the violated rights of your child? Take these steps before taking action:

1. Get the facts from your child, all the facts. Give your child plenty of time to tell the entire story. Ask pertinent questions. You need to know as many details as possible in order to get a complete picture. Questions that might assist you in getting the full story are these:

- Has anything like this happened before? Where? When? With whom?

- Who was there? What did they see/say/do?

- How do you think the other person was feeling?

- What caused that person to do or to say that thing?

- What did you do/say/think?

- Why did you react (or not react) that way?

- Why do you think the other person reacted the way he/she did?

- What could you have done differently?

- What will you do differently next time?

- What do you think you should do now?

- What do you want me to do?

2. If it seems necessary, corroborate the facts. Ask another trusted and reliable person before flying into action. That other person might be a coach, a teacher, or another parent.

3. Avoid talking to another child without talking to the child's parent/guardian first. Children do not appreciate another child's parent approaching them about a relationship issue. The parents of the child may also be highly offended when this happens. The problem almost always escalates and may result in a permanent breach in the relationship between the families. Sadly, the children are the ones to suffer in the years that follow. I know of far too many cases where valuable childhood friendships were broken apart because of the unnecessary, overreacting interference of parents. The opening illustration in this chapter is a classic example of inappropriate parental involvement severing a valuable childhood friendship.

4. If at all possible, encourage your child to negotiate the problem with your guidance and counseling, but without your physical presence. Learning to be a successful negotiator is one of life's most important relationship skills. An elementary-age child is not only capable of beginning to learn this skill but is resilient enough to learn very quickly and experience immediate benefit.

Learning to negotiate difficult situations and bring them to a satisfactory resolution is certain to raise your child's confidence level. Effective, peaceable confrontation is a tremendous asset to anyone. This life skill can begin to be learned at an early age, particularly if the parent is a skillful negotiator.

5. Step in if necessary. If, after taking these steps, you and your child are certain that it is in your child's best interests to intervene, then do so. Naturally, it is best to wait until your emotions are under control before you advance into unknown territory on behalf of your child. Of course you want to be the heroic defender of your child. However, it is still wise to model self-control for your child—to be the responsible adult your admiring child is watching and desires to emulate.

Parental intervention may be mandatory in some instances. If a child is being bullied, and the parent witnesses the incident, it may be necessary to intervene immediately for the safety of your child. This is particularly true when the incident happens in a neighborhood setting and if you are the sole authority figure who witnesses the incident. Bullies need to be stopped, for their good and for the good of their victims.

Some children are helpless because of age, size, maturation, or any one of a number of disabilities. In such cases, a parent will often need to step into a situation more quickly than otherwise would be necessary or wise.

One Girl's Lessons

The third-grade girl was quiet and shy at school but

outgoing at home. She was a good student. Her parents firmly believed in "doing your best at all times." The girl was expected to earn good grades, which she did.

The child felt that the teacher did not like her. She told her mother, who simply stated, "Not everyone in life will like you."

As the school year proceeded, the girl felt that the teacher was making fun of her artwork in front of the others in the class. Art was the child's weakest subject. When the girl complained, her mother responded, "You must learn to accept criticism and continue to do the best you can."

One day, the increasingly shy girl did something in class to anger the teacher. What it was the child said she did not know, but the girl still remembers the teacher giving her long hair a hard, angry pull, which hurt on the outside but far more on the inside.

The girl cried to her mother, who calmly said, "For the rest of your life you will be meeting people who are difficult. You must learn to deal with them and with the situations that arise, and besides, the year will soon be over, and you will have a different teacher."

What effect did that early situation have on the confidence level of the child? What was knowingly or unknowingly communicated to the girl was this:

- Her mother was not going to stand up for her.

- Her mother would defend the authority figure, no matter what.

- It would do no good to go to her mother in the future with her complaints about people in charge.

- She must accept the treatment of the authority figure and show respect for the position, even if she felt the person was wrong.

How do I know that those were the things that the
little girl learned? I am that little girl. Obviously, the
incident had an impact on my life to be remembered
so clearly.

Through the years, there were other incidents. My
mother's responses did not change. Looking back, I
believe that my mother may have been guilty of underreacting. In such a situation she should have come
to my defense. But I also derived a special benefit that
has helped me through my entire life. I learned at an
early age to run to God with my woes, sorrows, and
complaints. I discovered that God was always there to
listen and to comfort. I began to know a little of the
magnificent, unconditional love of God. I began to
learn to get my confidence from God, rather than from
a person, even though that person might be my mother
who loved me dearly and wanted the best for me.

I share this example to illustrate that parents make
mistakes. We are human beings. We can be guilty of
overreacting or underreacting. Likewise, our children
put their own interpretations on what we do and say.
One child may benefit from what a parent says while
another child might be bruised by the same treatment.
When we do bruise our children, we can ask their forgiveness.

A sixth grader relates this story. "It really helps my
confidence level when my parents admit to making a
mistake. My parents thought I did something wrong,
and blamed me, and punished me. Later on they found
out that I was telling the truth. They said they were
sorry. I forgave them. I think that helped their confidence and mine."

2

"My Child Can't Handle that Kind of Responsibility"

"Confidence is knowing you can do something."
—*Fourth grader*

"Confidence is believing in yourself and feeling that you are not under too much pressure in what you do."
—*Fifth grader*

The single parent of a fourth-grade boy called the office with a simple request. The mother had neglected to give the boy money to purchase a hot lunch. This is not an unusual problem. When a student forgets to bring a lunch or lunch money, the school routinely provides "The Office Special," a nourishing, inexpensive "no frills" lunch and charges the parent on the following month's statement.

The mother hesitated for a moment and then made her decision. "I'll come with the lunch money between shifts. Please let him wait in the office in case I'm late."

Shortly after the boy's lunch time began, the mother dashed into the office, gave the boy his money, apologized about forgetting, kissed him, and nearly collided with me as she raced out.

I was curious. What dire emergency had brought her to school in the middle of her demanding workday? A fourth grader's forgotten lunch money! I decided to ask some questions.

I was aware that this boy was on full scholarship. A retired couple who knew and loved the mom had chosen to provide for the son's education. I also knew that the mom worked several jobs just to maintain a modest lifestyle. The boy's father had little part in their life, financially or otherwise.

I discovered that the boy purchased a hot lunch each day because he did not like what his mother fixed and didn't want to eat it. She also knew he would not be pleased with the Office Special.

The boy, the mother, and I had a conference. The boy was able to calculate the monthly cost of the lunches, figure out how many hours his mother worked to pay for the lunches, and determine what other things could have been done with the money. The boy made a surprising discovery! He and his mom could have gone to Disneyland two or three times a year for what the lunches cost!

When I asked, "Why aren't you making your own lunches?" the boy shrugged. Neither he nor his mother had thought of that.

How Much Can They Do?

Of course this fourth-grade boy was more than capable of making his own lunch. For him it would have been a simple responsibility and only one of many that he could do to assist his mother and work together toward common goals.

Why are some loving, sincere, hard-working parents reluctant to allow their children to assume responsibilities that the children are capable of handling?

"I want my child to know how much I love him. Doing this for him is one way I can show my love."

It is common for a parent involved in a divorce or

a custody battle to overindulge a child in the name of love. The parent is afraid, and with good reason.

- The child might be taken away.

- The child might choose to live with the other parent.

- The child might appear to love the other parent more.

The mom in this story was fearful. When she attempted to discipline, the boy said he didn't love her and wanted to live with his father. Children are smart. They know exactly how, when, and where to press our panic buttons.

Teaching a child a skill and encouraging a child to strive toward a goal are strong, practical ways to show love for the child as well as to build the child's confidence. The mom and boy in this story began to work together as a team. The boy assumed the responsibility of making his lunches. He and his mom kept track of the money saved each day. They celebrated at Disneyland when enough was saved.

That mom showed great love for the child in allowing him to learn some basic financial principles along with mastery of simple meal preparation.

In answering the question, "What should a parent do to build a child's confidence," a third grader wrote, "Parents should tell their children to make goals for themselves."

A sixth grader expressed it this way: "A parent should help their child with something they are having trouble with and encourage them to build confidence. My mom helped me with my math when I was having trouble."

The highly respected writer and therapist T. L.

Brink speaks bluntly. "Pampering a child is equivalent to teaching him that he is too weak or incompetent to do things for himself. Therefore, he never develops a sense of realistic accomplishment."

"It's just easier to do it myself."

How many times have you thought or said, "It's easier to do it myself." That's for sure! Especially in the early years! I still remember when my own children wanted to help Mommy. The task took about three times as long and had to be redone over and over. I can well understand why moms wait for a child's naptime or bedtime so that they can do the necessary household tasks without "help" from their adorable and eager but totally unskilled labor!

But what about building the confidence level of the child? Is the sacrifice of time, patience, and energy worth the effort? If your goal is to raise a confident child, the answer must be a resounding yes.

This training period is particularly frustrating for the parent. Precisely when your time and energy are at a premium, your children are so teachable. This is the time to *Carpe Diem*—"seize the day" or "make the most of the moment"!

I clearly remember my eighteen month old and three year old wanting to help Mommy wash windows. Of course I wanted them to learn to wash windows but not now! I was in a hurry and had no time for nonsense. What to do with these eager faces and willing workers? I filled a couple of spray bottles with water, gave them a towel, and we began to work. How could I encourage and not discourage them from wanting to help, build their confidence, and yet not have the smeariest windows in the city?

I believe that God gave some acceptable words that served the purpose for that day and the years that followed. I simply told the children that Mommy would put on the finishing touches to their job. They accepted this, as I essentially redid their work, and yet they were affirmed in their sweet, childish efforts. This technique worked as the children learned to do the simple chores of childhood such as making their beds and cleaning their rooms. As time went by, I really was merely putting on the finishing touches. In later years, they would let me know when they were ready for me to give the "once over" in checking their well-performed task. This always gave me the opportunity to praise and to give a suggestion for improvement, if necessary.

Responding to Mistakes

It is interesting that children are particularly vocal in their belief that a parent destroys their confidence by screaming when they attempt to help but make mistakes. I can imagine the frustration of this mother, as well as the hurt of this fourth grader who wrote:

> One night I tried to do the wash as a favor. But I didn't know what I was doing. My mom was upset and started to scream. Her best skirt was ruined. I think if she would have had more temperance she wouldn't have screamed. I felt like running away. I hid behind the dresser. But I came out because I was hungry.[1]

I would like to think that after the mom calmed down, she apologized and began to teach the child how to properly do a wash. Obviously, the child had demonstrated a desire to learn, even though the initial result was disastrous.

Soichiro Honda, businessman and CEO of Honda

Corporation, said, "To me, success can be achieved only through repeated failure and introspection. In fact, success represents the 1 percent of your work that results from 99 percent that is called failure."[2]

It was one thing to have my daughter help Mommy in the kitchen in the early years. But, as a teenager, she wanted to learn to prepare meals all by herself. This sounded good to her. After all, she felt she had the skills necessary from all of her years of assisting. We established the ground rules:

- I needed to approve the menu.

- She would make the grocery list to include all necessary ingredients not in the house.

- If her schedule and mine permitted, she would shop for the groceries.

- If she ran out of anything currently in the house because of her menu, she would put it on the grocery list for the following week.

- She was responsible for cleaning up any and all messes.

On paper, the idea sounded infallible. In practice, allowing her to be responsible for the entire meal was a timing nightmare at first. The family would expect dinner at 7:00 P.M. Oops. Her first few attempts tested the patience and self-control of a hungry family.

What did we do? Waited patiently (that was the hardest part for me). Asked if she needed or wanted help. Waited some more. It was not easy. What was the ultimate result? After several shaky attempts, our family was blessed with a teenager who had the confidence to plan a complete dinner, prepare the meal, and clean up following the meal.

Children are like us. They will fail repeatedly when trying to learn. Does that mean we should do the task for them?

→ A fifth grader cautions parents, "The parent should help. They should not yell at the child like, 'why can't you get it right?'"

→ A fourth grader adds, "They shouldn't say 'Oh, you'll never be able to do that.' They should encourage but not do it for them."

→ A fifth grader explains, "If that child has to write a report the parent shouldn't tell them what to write because then the child won't have confidence."

Children need us to come alongside with encouragement and patience, treating them the way we like to be treated when something is difficult but necessary to learn. The result will be a child growing in ability and confidence, and in love, appreciation, and trust for the parent.

"I'm not sure my child is ready for that."

Children differ greatly in their developmental abilities. Some children are ready to assume responsibility at a younger age than others. Children develop at different rates, and some children mature much more slowly than others.

Developmental age is the age at which a child is behaving as a total person—the child's level of functioning. The developmental components that contribute to the functioning age of a child are physical, mental, spiritual, social, and emotional. In Luke 2:52

(NASB) Scripture assures us that Jesus developed in each of these five areas. We are told that Jesus developed "in wisdom" . . . mentally, "stature". . . physically, "in favor with God". . . spiritually, and in favor "with men". . . socially and emotionally.

A child might very well be functioning at six, or even at a seven-year-old level, mentally, but a composite of the *whole* development might place the child at a five-year-old level of functioning. Illness, divorce, death in the family, moving, having a birthday just before the school cutoff date, premature birth, or any one of a number of physical, mental, emotional, or social differences will affect the developmental age of a child.

Another reason for the huge variety of developmental abilities among children is that some parents begin to train children to be responsible at younger ages than other parents who are more hesitant.

It is wise for a parent to find out what responsibilities are being expected or not expected of other children of the same age and stage as your child. This questioning will provide a guideline for you to make appropriate decisions. Checking with your child's pediatrician and teachers, as well as with friends you respect, will help to provide a framework.

If you find that most other parents have higher expectations and requirements for their child than you do for yours, ask yourself these questions: Am I trying to overprotect or control my child? Do I want a child who is completely dependent on me?

Honest answers to these questions will give clues as to what you need to do in the future. Remember that the goal is to raise a confident child.

Kari Czer is a mother with seven children between the ages of three and fifteen. She has no household help nor does she have the luxury of grandparents or extended family. Yet she is able to do some substitute teaching "with advance notice." Her husband is the medical director of the heart transplant program at Cedars Sinai Medical Center in Los Angeles. He is also the director of transplantation cardiology cardio- thoracic surgery at Cedars Sinai. In addition to this, he is a full professor of medicine at UCLA. Obviously, he is an extraordinarily busy man with a highly de- manding schedule.

People who have been to their home at different times, sometimes unexpectedly, indicate that it is or- ganized and clean. How is this possible? Kari smiles, laughs, and says, "It isn't always!" However, she and her husband believe that "teaching children to accept responsibility for their behavior and upholding God's standard is a must for maintaining family harmony, productivity, and successful Christian living."

I asked Kari to explain the organization of such a huge household. Without hesitation, she said, "The children have to learn how to be a part of the everyday responsibilities. I could never do it alone. I don't have the time, and I don't have the strength." The Czer Family Chore Charts are included as samples to illus- trate what is expected of these children and how she has organized the duties.

THE CZER FAMILY'S WEEKDAY TO-DO LIST

	Monday	Tuesday	Wednesday	Thursday	Friday
Peter, 15	sweep clean counters school work piano practice personal Bible study	empty dishwasher clean foyer school work piano practice personal Bible study	set & clear table clean shoes school work piano practice personal Bible study	laundry & pick up school work piano practice personal Bible study	make lunches clean car school work piano practice personal Bible study
Luke, 14	make lunches clean car school work piano practice personal Bible study	sweep clean counters school work piano practice personal Bible study	empty dishwasher clean foyer school work piano practice personal Bible study	set & clear table clean shoes school work piano practice personal Bible study	laundry & pick up school work piano practice personal Bible study
Laurel, 12	laundry pick up school work piano practice personal Bible study	make lunches clean car school work piano practice personal Bible study	sweep clean counters school work piano practice personal Bible study	empty dishwasher clean foyer school work piano practice personal Bible study	set & clear table clean shoes school work piano practice personal Bible study

	Monday	Tuesday	Wednesday	Thursday	Friday
Andrew, 11	set & clear table clean shoes school work piano practice personal Bible study	laundry & pick up school work piano practice personal Bible study	make lunches clean car school work piano practice personal Bible study	sweep clean counters school work piano practice personal Bible study	empty dishwasher clean foyer school work piano practice personal Bible study
Christa, 9	empty dishwasher clean foyer school work piano practice personal Bible study	set & clear table clean shoes school work piano practice personal Bible study	laundry & pick up school work piano practice personal Bible study	make lunches clean car school work piano practice personal Bible study	sweep clean counters school work piano practice personal Bible study
Paul, 6	make bed pick up room (toys & clothes) personal hygiene dress himself	make bed pick up room (clothes & toys) personal hygiene dress self	make bed pick up room (toys & clothes) personal hygiene dress self	make bed pick up room (clothes & toys) personal hygiene dress self	make bed pick up room (clothes & toys) personal hygiene dress self
Adam, 3* *with assistance	make bed pick up room (clothes & toys) personal hygiene dress self	make bed pick up room (clothes & toys) personal hygiene dress self	make bed pick up room (clothes & toys) personal hygiene dress self	make bed pick up room (clothes & toys) personal hygiene dress self	make bed pick up room (clothes & toys) personal hygiene dress self

THE CZER FAMILY WEEKEND TO-DO LIST

	Weekend 1	Weekend 2	Weekend 3	Weekend 4
Peter, 15	change sheets clean hallways vacuum living room vacuum study	change sheets clean master bedroom vacuum living room vacuum study	change sheets clean downstairs bathroom vacuum living room vacuum study	change sheets clean kids' bathroom vacuum living room vacuum study
Luke, 14	change sheets clean kids' bathroom vacuum dining room vacuum den	change sheets clean hallways vacuum dining room vacuum den	change sheets clean master bedroom vacuum dining room vacuum den	change sheets clean downstairs bathroom vacuum dining room vacuum den
Laurel, 12	change sheets clean downstairs bathroom vacuum master bedroom	change sheets clean kids' bathroom vacuum master bedroom	change sheets clean hallways vacuum master bedroom	change sheets clean master bedroom vacuum master bedroom

	Weekend 1	Weekend 2	Weekend 3	Weekend 4
Andrew, 11	change sheets clean master bedroom vacuum stairs vacuum 1 bedroom	change sheets clean downstairs bathroom vacuum stairs vacuum 1 bedroom	change sheets clean kids' bathroom vacuum stairs vacuum 1 bedroom	change sheets clean hallways vacuum stairs vacuum 1 bedroom
Christa, 9	laundry vacuum 2 bedrooms	laundry vacuum 2 bedrooms	laundry vacuum 2 bedrooms	laundry vacuum 2 bedrooms
Paul, 6	make bed pick up room (clothes & toys) personal hygiene dress self	make bed pick up room (clothes & toys) personal hygiene dress self	make bed pick up room (clothes & toys) personal hygiene dress self	make bed pick up room (clothes & toys) personal hygiene dress self
Adam, 3* *with assistance	make bed pick up room (clothes & toys) personal hygiene dress self	make bed pick up room (clothes & toys) personal hygiene dress self	make bed pick up room (clothes & toys) personal hygiene dress self	make bed pick up room (clothes & toys) personal hygiene dress self

Many families have found that charts that list and/or illustrate the household chores expected of their children provide helpful, nonverbal reminders. Some charts give space for the children to mark with a sticker or a pen when a certain task is completed each day.

Each time a task is learned and mastered, the confidence of the child grows. As the child continues to accept responsibility for doing the task, regardless of how mundane and mechanical it becomes, the character quality of responsibility grows.

A fourth grader wisely writes, "Confidence is thinking you can do something without doubting. Parents should encourage the child and tell them a story as if they weren't confident and now they have the strength to do it and God could help them again. I think God is helping my parents and me get more confident."

A fifth-grade girl adds a practical suggestion. "A parent should help by helping their children to do something that they want to do but are a little afraid to do. Example: Let's say a little girl wanted to take dancing lessons but was afraid that she might mess up and get embarrassed. Her parents should tell her that even if she does mess up she could always just do it again, and then after making sure she wanted to do it sign her up."

"My child likes to have me do this for him."

There is no doubt that loving parents want to do things for their children and that the children love to be served. This is necessary and appropriate. This serving only becomes dangerous when the balance is lost, and the parent continues to do things for the child that the child is able to do for himself, and should be doing for himself.

Overprotection of the child, which creates undue dependency on the parent, can cripple a child's confidence and prevent him or her from reaching God-given potential. Although letting go of control can be threatening to a well-meaning but compulsive mother, certain risks must be tolerated if a child is to progress into confidence.

A mature third grader wrote, "Since a parent can't always be there for the child, the parent should train a child to pray for confidence in God. Parents should teach children by reading his Holy Word to have faith in God."

- James Dobson says in *Hide or Seek,* "The parental purpose should be to grant increasing freedom and responsibility year by year, so that when the child gets beyond adult control, he will no longer need it."

- Responsible parents desire to rear children who become mature adults. A dear friend, Pat McIntyre, shares a superb quote from Abigail Van Buren: "My Definition of Maturity: The ability to stick with a job without being supervised, the ability to carry money without spending it, and the ability to bear an injustice without wanting to get even!" Perhaps this quote could also be entitled, "The Dream of Every Parent with Grown Children."

"I want to support my child's interests. There isn't time for everything."

The huge emphasis on participation in sports today frequently conflicts with classroom responsibilities. Some children in elementary school are involved in many different sports leagues throughout the year, sometimes participating in several leagues with the same sport during the same season. The consuming priority of sports has escalated tremendously over the past decade. No doubt the gargantuan salaries paid to sports figures and the idolizing of their celebrity status have contributed to this passion. Parents want their children to excel, and the children are eager.

Unfortunately, there are many times when the children simply do not have the time to devote to classroom studies, which then must take a back seat to sports. Schools are faced with parents who resent the homework that may detract from the time spent on the playing field. The parents gladly choose the responsibilities associated with playing the sport, but don't wish to inflict the classroom responsibilities on their child. This becomes particularly passionate in the area of homework. Some sport-enthusiast parents cry, "The school needs to lighten up on the homework. My child is tired when he gets home at 8:30 or 9:00 at night from sports practice. He doesn't have time to study." That's true.

For these parents, the responsibilities involving sports are just and fair, but classroom responsibilities are too much. "It's more than my child can handle. The school needs to change." Those of us involved in education for many years find such comments intriguing. Private schools today are merely trying to maintain the academic standards of a decade ago.

Wayne Gretzky, "The Great One," as he has been known since he was a child, holds 62 National Hockey League offensive records. Included are the most career goals (885), most assists (1,910), and most total points—goals and assists combined—(2,795).

His father, Walter, was his coach and was crucial to his development as a player. He had Wayne practicing stick-handling with tennis balls during the summer. The spinning bounce of the tennis balls refined his responses, allowing him to bat flying pucks out of the air with his stick. Despite endless repetition, Gretzky never grew bored with drills. He had a singular focus that allowed him to practice relentlessly.

When Gretzky was in elementary school, he'd skate from 7:00 A.M. to 8:30 A.M., go to school, come home, do his homework, hit the ice again, and skate until his mother called him for dinner.

He'd eat while still wearing his skates. Then he'd go back out and skate until time for bed.

Curiously, his parents made sure that hockey wasn't his sole focus. They taught him discipline and showed him what was important—they made him finish his homework before he could play hockey. If you do well in school, his father told him, that focus can help you succeed in sports. Gretzky was an A student all through school.[3]

It is vital that parents be responsible to set priorities for their children. Children need the daily discipline of doing homework and doing it correctly in order to survive with confidence in the adult world. Like it or not, the disciplines of academics are generally more useful than sports training to 99 percent of all people when they go to hunt for a job in our increasingly technological society.

The nineteenth-century scientist Thomas Huxley said it best,

> Perhaps the most valuable result of all education is the ability to make yourself do the thing you have to do when it ought to be done, whether you like it or not. It is the first lesson that ought to be learned, and however early a man's training begins, it is probably the last lesson that he learns thoroughly.

A parent who genuinely desires to raise a confident, responsible child must be willing to make some costly sacrifices. A parent must give up time, energy, convenience, and must also relinquish control as the child becomes more and more confident, capable, and independent. The playwright Sidney Howard said it well. "One-half of knowing what you want is knowing what you must give up before you get it."

3

"I Must Protect My Child from the Outside World"

"Confidence is when you think you should do or not do something but you are scared. God can give you confidence to say yes or no."
—*Fourth grader*

"Confidence is being able to speak up boldly for what you think is right and not to be afraid of doing it."
—*Sixth grader*

Reading, listening, or watching the news for one month is enough to inject fear into the heart of any conscientious parent who is trying to instill God-based character qualities into his or her children. Where are the safe havens? We have all heard stories of atrocities coming out of the best neighborhoods, malls, schools, camps, churches, as well as carefully sponsored athletic activities and social events.

Is the home even a safe place? Moral pollution can sneak into the finest home masked in a variety of disguises, in spite of the watchful care of a concerned parent. One accidental click on the Internet, an unfortunate flick of the radio, TV, or cable can sow seeds of corruption. An uncensored video has the power to mar the innocence of childhood.

It is also somewhat chilling to realize that the ages of five to twelve are vital decision-making years. At around seven or eight, children form their own concept of the world in which they live, and this concept stays with them for life. Research studies establish that eighty percent of a child's values and attitudes are established by the age of eight. This beautiful and thought-provoking poem captures the impressionableness of those early years:

> I took a piece of plastic clay
> And idly fashioned it one day
> And as my fingers pressed it still
> It moved and yielded at my will.
>
> I came again when days were past,
> The bit of clay was hard at last.
> The form I gave it, it still bore
> And I could change that form no more.
>
> I took a piece of living clay
> And gently formed it day by day
> And molded with God's power and art
> A young child's soft and yielding heart.
>
> I came again when years were gone.
> A man now I looked upon.
> And he that early impress wore
> And I could change him never more.
>
> Anonymous

Parents observe the moral decay around them and fear for the adverse effects that this pollution will have on the hearts and minds of their children during the impressionable years. In a spirit of righteous indignation, disappointed parents pack up their children and belongings and head for a "better" place where things are "different," where the world will be safer for their family, where things are "the way they used to be." Who can blame them? We all understand the pursuit of security and happiness.

Coming to Terms with the World

Occasionally, a family is fortunate enough to achieve their dream. More often, parents come to terms with the fact that evil and decadence permeate the land as well as the human heart. It's futile to flee. Our Lord Jesus does not provide a way of escape from the world. He spoke to the Father in John 17:15: "I pray not that you should take them out of the world, but that you should keep them from the evil one." Parents are polarized as to how to respond.

Some parents respond by trying to *shelter* their children from the unpleasant realities of the world. One such mother approached her son's teacher with a concerned look. She needed to share something with the teacher as soon as possible. The teacher wanted to deal with whatever the problem was immediately. The mother spoke with intensity. "Please do not use the 'D' word in front of my son. He does not know what that word means, and I do not want him to know. He is too young."

The teacher searched her mind for the "D" word. Nothing came. She asked the mother to either spell or tell her what the "D" word was. The mother looked around, then whispered, "Divorce." The skilled teacher kept her composure and gently informed the aghast mother that her nine-year-old son appeared to not only know the "D" word but also know what it meant.

Other parents respond by trying to *deny* that the sin of the world has affected their children. When accused of using inappropriate language on the playground, a fourth grader's parents said that this must not be true because, "We know every word he's ever heard, and he has never heard that one."

Still other parents valiantly attempt to *block out* the sin of the world to keep their children pure. Such parents are vehemently opposed to drug abuse prevention programs, believing that such knowledge will only serve to incite kids' curiosity and may even lead to experimentation.

Responding with Balance

These extreme examples are not infrequent among conscientious parents who are striving to rear children that are "in the world but not of the world." There are several points to consider that will help to bring balance into this delicate and emotionally charged issue and will contribute to building confidence in your children.

1. Answer your child's questions. Always be honest but avoid giving more information than is necessary for the age and stage of the child. This is especially true where questions of sex are involved. Parents frequently overload a child with too many details and facts that are not necessary to adequately and honestly answer the question.

2. Filter what the child sees, hears, and listens to as much as is reasonable during the early years. The parent must also realize that even the most protected child will see and/or hear things that are not what the parent would choose. A close relative, neighbor, or friend's family member may be the one to use offensive language or live a lifestyle that is abhorrent to the parent. By keeping the lines of communication open, the child will have the freedom to share and ask questions without fear. This turns a potentially polluting situation into a teaching tool for the parent and a valuable learning opportunity for the child. Such a typical predicament is a powerful way of training children to accept, love, pray for, and show grace to people who live and act in ways that are unacceptable to them, without being influenced by their behaviors. Many a relative and/or friend has come to know God because of the gracious attitudes of family and friends faithfully demonstrated over a long period of time.

My uncle came to Christ after our family had prayed for him for years. In spite of his seeming delight in using language that offended and telling repulsive stories in front of our children, we continued to love him, pray for him, and attend family gatherings. This was a wonderful practical lesson for our children. They were exposed to "the world" with us present. This ugly circumstance provided us with fantastic opportunities to talk and to pray together as a concerned family. Ultimate good came from it.

3. Assume the responsibility to know your child's friends. One way that a parent can do this positively is to encourage your child to have friends visit. The parent can then listen and observe, and will be able to determine which friendships to encourage with more visits and which to discourage.

In the case of my own children, this method led to inviting friends to be a part of family vacations, as well as many weekends and holidays through the years.

4. Be realistic. Parents who "expect" that their children will never disobey or cause embarrassment and humiliation are parents who are going to be continually surprised and disappointed. Children need training. Should a parent "expect" to be obeyed? Definitely. Should a parent lose heart or confidence when disobedience occurs? Never. Children come into the world ready to be naughty. Scripture assures us of that sad fact. In Jeremiah 17:9 we read, "The heart is deceitful above all things and desperately wicked" (NKJV). Deal with each situation as it occurs, praying for love, good judgment, patience, and consistency.

5. Be a role model by admitting mistakes, accepting responsibility for error, asking forgiveness from God and from the individual (often your own child). Then model moving forward with confidence, asking God to help you strengthen the area of weakness. Nothing will penetrate the heart of your children more than the genuine humility of parents before God and before the offended individual.

Let your children know of your personal struggles with temptation. After all, our children know when we are angry, critical, unforgiving, or indulging in gossip, so we might as well be honest with them. This is another way of keeping communication open and honest in the family.

6. Diffuse power struggles before they begin. When a household is full of tension due to constant power struggles, kids are tempted to disobey. Sometimes a child who really wants to obey is goaded into wrongdoing by a power struggle set up by a parent. I have found that the best way to avoid such struggles is to give kids choices, beginning with simple choices like the choice between shirts and ending with the many choices available for an older teen. *Don't Give In, Give Choices,* which I wrote with Dr. Grace Ketterman, gives more information on this extremely important aspect of building confidence and mutual respect with your child.

7. Create an environment of trust. If you have laid the foundation of right thinking and acting in the heart of your child during the formative years, you must entrust more freedom to the child with each passing year. Naturally, more freedom for the child means more responsibility. If and when trust is broken, the child will lose the freedom and appropriate consequences must follow.

What about Schooling?

Some parents consider that their most important choice related to "the world" is their choice of schooling. Parents painfully agonize over the right educational choice for their children: public schooling, private secular schooling, private religious schooling, homeschooling. Each choice has advantages and disadvantages. Each choice has critics and supporters. In some cases, the supporters become highly emotional and so full of zeal that they condemn all the rest. I have actually observed how this misplaced missionary zeal has split families and severed friendships. I don't believe this is what God intends for his children.

In reality, a certain educational choice may be right for one child or for one family for a period of time, while a different choice may be best at another time for another child or another family. The parental motivation is an important factor to analyze before making an educational choice. If you are wondering what to do, consider these questions as you prayerfully make your decision.

- Are you making this decision as a family unit?

- What is the time frame for your decision? It is wise to evaluate your decision for each of your children every year.

- Are you being pressured by friends or extended family to make a particular educational choice?

- Are financial pressures influencing your decision?

- Are driving/time pressures influencing your decision?

- Is this decision in your child's best interest or for your own convenience?

- Have you fully explored all your educational options?

- What type of schooling does your child want and why? Are the reasons consistent with your family goals and values?

- Will this choice help your child to achieve full academic, emotional, and/or spiritual development? List specifics.

- Could this choice possibly hinder your child's academic, emotional, and/or spiritual development? List specifics.

- Do you have the confidence in your decision to stand alone among your friends or extended family?

You and your children must visit the various types of schools to know exactly what happens in the classroom and on the playground. You will learn more from a visit to the campus than you will from listening to comments and observations of friends. Bring questions with you. Write the answers down so that you can refer to them at a later time. Revisit schools, if necessary, to help clarify your selection. You need to have peace of mind and heart when making this all-important decision for your family. Do not be embarrassed to call schools to get further information. After all, this decision affects your family's future.

As an administrator of a **private Christian** elementary school, I can assure you that there are as many different types of Christian schools as there are varieties of Christian churches. Each has its own unique personality and distinctives, with corresponding advantages and disadvantages. Visiting the schools you are considering, asking questions, and praying for the Lord's direction will help you to make the selection that is best for your family.

My husband and I wrongly assumed that our children would continue in Christian schools through high school. Christian junior high and high school was the correct choice for our daughter but not for our son. He expressed a desire to go to a **private secular school** in our area. It is ranked as one of the top three preparatory schools in the nation. Everything about the idea staggered us—the tuition, the commute, the non-Christian environment. Our family prayerfully considered the questions listed above, one by one. In time, the individual answers came. To our amazement, he did attend that prep school from seventh through twelfth grade. It was definitely the right choice.

Richard Grant is the President and Headmaster of Advantage Preparatory School, Inc. APS provides a **homeschooling** network center and currently has 270 students enrolled. Richard has been involved with homeschooling since 1987. I asked Richard, a respected friend for many years, to share from his perspective.

I think the incredible growth that we see in family-based education [homeschooling] can be attributed to the failure of traditional education in three major areas: values, academics, and socialization. . . . [Parents] are realizing that they are ultimately responsible, before God, for the education and well-being of their children. As these parents examine the traditional providers of education, they find they can no longer delegate this critical responsibility to them.

Grant says that one of the most important reasons that parents choose not to homeschool is due to time constraints. Homeschooling requires a great deal of time and energy, and some parents do not have enough of either. For example, families that require two incomes usually do not feel that they can homeschool. However, the book *Homeschooling on a Shoestring* by Judith Waite Allee and Melissa Morgan offers parents options for homeschooling even if both parents currently work outside the home.

Debbie and John Bickford are long-time friends I hold in high esteem. They have worked in **public schools** for over twenty years. They have been involved in teaching and in administration. They chose to give their children a Christian school education through elementary school, and then move them to public schools. They share their point of view.

Because we know the good, the bad, and the ugly of public schooling, the decision was possibly more difficult for us. Although we want to protect our children from the evil of our world, we want them to develop the strength of character that battles on the front line will give them. We believe they cannot develop strength for the major moral battles of life without experiencing daily victories in the small character skirmishes. . . . We believe it is good for the children to be exposed gradually to the world system in a way that allows for maximum parental interaction and encouragement.

John Skidmore is a public school history teacher who grew up in a home that actively encouraged impurity. He is an excellent example of the redeeming love and grace of God. He adds these thought-provoking remarks to the discussion of relating to the world:

> There is a great deal of sentimentalism about innocence today. There is no power in innocence. Innocence is not a virtue and is not a substitute for purity. Too often, innocence is our modern, watered-down substitute for purity. Innocence is merely a vacuum to be filled with something later. God, our good Father, doesn't allow us to go through life without being tempted, because he knows what he wants to produce. What God wants is to make pure men and women, not innocent ones. Purity is different from innocence in that it understands evil, knows the force of it, and yet rejects it and chooses the right. . . . The role of the parent is to direct and to guide into what is good, and to model it, so that the child can make informed decisions. [It is] not to take the decision away from the child, because the ability to decide is what the parent should be instilling in the child.

No matter what form of schooling parents choose, professionals, parents, and children all agree that the parents, not the school, are the biggest influence on the young child.

Charles Kingsley, an English novelist and clergyman of the 1800s, said it well: "Nothing is so infectious in the life of a child as the example of the parent." Albert Einstein also put it succinctly. "The only rational way of educating is to be an example."

Parents have the power in the early years to form the worldview of the child.

→ Parents want their children to be readers.
Question: Do the parents read?

→ Parents do not want their children to be bigots.
Question: Do the children hear the parents make prejudicial remarks and generalizations?

→ Parents want their children to memorize Scripture.
Question: Do the parents quote the Bible from memory? How many portions of Scripture have the parents memorized recently?

→ Parents want their children to be willing workers.
Question: Do the parents moan and groan about their work?

→ Parents want their children to be dependable and responsible.
Question: Can your children count on you to say what you mean and mean what you say?

→ Parents want their children to be kind.
Question: Are the parents kind to each other? to their children? to friends and strangers?

→ Parents want to raise children with self-control.
Question: How many times in the past month have the children seen the parents "lose it" over something?

→ Parents want to raise honest children.
Question: How many times in the past four weeks have the children known the parents to lie in some way, shape, or form?

Perhaps more than any other actor, Jimmy Stewart embodied the all-American values he portrayed in films such as *Mr. Smith Goes to Washington* and *It's a Wonderful Life*. Those were values he learned from his father, a hardware store owner. A priority for Alexander Stewart was to turn his son into a fine man and an outstanding citizen.

"I was always at my Dad's side, whenever possible, observing all that I could about ethics and morals that would set the pattern for my life," Jimmy Stewart once said. His father was a volunteer fireman and often took Jimmy along when he was serving the community. There, Jimmy learned the virtues of serving simply to do good.

Stewart credits his father for teaching him to think for himself. "My father prided himself on letting me make my own decision, but I also had to accept responsibility for that decision." For example, although Stewart's parents feared for his life when he decided to try flying, they realized the importance of letting him pursue his ambition. Jimmy saved every penny he got working at his family's hardware store until he had enough saved to try.

That experience confirmed his desire to be a flier. Stewart promised himself he'd be a fighter pilot if America ever went to war, and he prepared for that possibility. He got the necessary credentials, logging more than 400 flying hours in the 1930s. Based on that experience, Stewart applied for a commission as an Army Air Force pilot. After he was accepted, he immediately began an extensive schedule of flight training and ground school class work.

Stewart's war record included twenty combat missions as a command pilot. After being promoted to squadron commander, he became operations officer. From 1944–45, he served as chief of staff, 2nd Combat Wing, 2nd Division, 8th Air Force. When Stewart was taxed by the pressure of leadership, he turned to his spirituality. He learned to lean on the words of a tattered copy of the Psalms his father had given him.

He recalled one particular night when his group had suffered heavy casualties during the day.

> I led my squadron out again, deep into enemy territory. Imagination can be a soldier's worst enemy. Fear is an insidious and deadly thing; it can warp judgment, freeze reflexes, and breed mistakes. Worse, it's contagious. I knew my own fear, if not checked, could infect my crew members, and I could feel it growing in me.
>
> I remembered talking to my father when I was a boy and asking him about his experiences in both wars he served in. I had asked him if he'd ever been afraid. He said, "Every man is, son, but just remember you can't handle fear all by yourself. Give it to God. He'll carry it for you."
>
> I reread the 91st Psalm that my father had given me when I left, and I felt comforted, felt that I had done all I could.
>
> The psalm reads, in part: "He that dwelleth in the secret place of the most high shall abide under the shadow of the Almighty. I will say of the Lord, He is my refuge and my fortress; my God; in him will I trust."[4]

Jimmy Stewart is an individual whose father's early example permeated the man his son became. Because of his father's role model, Jimmy Stewart was able to take "the high road." He was "in the world, but not of the world."

4

"I Should Try to Make Life Fair for My Child"

"Confidence is when things aren't fair, and you still feel OK inside."
—Sixth grader

"I think confidence can be when you play your best, and you still lose, or worse yet when you are not picked."
—Sixth grader

The father of the sixth-grade boy was extremely upset. He was vehemently opposed to how the boys' coach was handling the after-school league. "It's not fair, and it needs to be changed."

When we met together, the boys' coach explained that his son barely made the team and was not a strong player. The boys were told at try-outs that the emphasis would be on using the strongest players the majority of the time. When the school team made it to the league sectionals, the coach did what he said. He played the stronger players the majority of the time. It was true that the son sat on the bench for most of the games.

The father angrily disputed the competitive emphasis. "My boy has shown up for practice, just like the other boys. It is not fair that each of the players don't get equal time to play in the games."

The athletic director explained that during the regular Physical Education period, the goal is to encourage each child and give every child equal opportunity, but that was not true in the competitive league play. There were try-outs to see if a boy could make the team, and there were no guarantees that each player would be used equally.

The father's position did not change. "If that is the unfair way you are going to run the league, my child will never participate in after-school sports again." And he never did.

It was clear that life was only fair when the son was given the recognition the father thought he should have in each activity in which the boy chose to participate. This boy's father reflected a prevailing sentiment of many of today's parents: "If my child can't be first, then it's not fair, and he will never play again!"

Curiously, the father never thought it was unfair when his son was chosen for lead parts in the Christmas productions year after year because of his excellent dramatic ability and fine singing voice. Other boys who tried out for the same parts were good, but not nearly as gifted in the areas of singing and drama.

Parents are naturally proud of their children and would like to have their child be the best athlete, the most outstanding student, and a star in the arts as well. With such a shower of talent and natural ability, the parents would live a life shining in the reflected glory of their child. Since no child is great at everything, parents are frequently tempted to try to elevate their child's performance by making things "fair and equal." What this really means is, "Nobody should be recognized as being better than my child."

Trying to make life fair for your child is endlessly frustrating, completely exhausting, and full of disappointment. Some parents persist in searching for fairness by changing schools on a regular basis in a futile attempt to find the one, true school that recognizes that their child is "outstanding."

Bishop Fulton J. Sheen has a thought-provoking comment on such ill-concealed pride. "Pride is an admission of weakness; it secretly fears all competition and dreads all rivals."

Life Isn't Fair

I was in first grade when I discovered that life was not fair. I made a "best friend." But then I got sick and was absent for over a week. When I came back, the little girl announced, "You're not my best friend anymore." That was that, and I had to learn to live with the pain of being rejected for no apparent reason.

While struggling to teach basic skills to a classroom of mentally retarded children in the public schools, I was struck daily with the unfairness of life. These children had done nothing wrong, and yet they were handicapped from birth for the remainder of their lives.

Is it fair that a young NFL athlete, although supremely gifted and presumably a nice person, should be awarded a seven-year, $42,000,000 package that includes an $11.5 million signing bonus? Is that seven-year contribution really worth more to society than that of a faithful mail carrier, a compassionate nurse, or a dedicated scientist?

Dr. Richard Carlson, consultant on stress and happiness, encourages us to "surrender to the fact that life isn't fair." The best-selling author explains further:

> One of the mistakes many of us make is that we feel sorry for ourselves, or for others, thinking that life should be fair, or that someday it will be. It's not and it won't [be]. One of the nice things about surrendering to the fact that life isn't fair

is that it keeps us from feeling sorry for ourselves by encouraging us to do the very best we can with what we have.

Surrendering to this fact also keeps us from feeling sorry for others because we are reminded that everyone is dealt a different hand, and everyone has unique strengths and challenges. This insight has helped me to deal with the problems of raising two children, the difficult decision I've had to make about who to help and who I can't help, as well as with my own personal struggles during those times that I have felt victimized or unfairly treated.[5]

Learning to accept the inevitable unfairness of life, our own limitations, as well as those of our children, can give peace and contentment. And this is one of life's greatest accomplishments!

Many times, life's most notable victories are achieved when an individual triumphs over the blatant unfairness of life. Recently the film world has thrilled at the courage of Christopher Reeve, who became a paraplegic after an equestrian accident. The handsome star did not give up or let the paralysis of self-pity immobilize his spirit. He has bravely overcome and has even been able to work as an actor once again.

Although football star Ricky Williams captured the Heisman trophy, college football's highest honor, by the fourth largest margin in the award's sixty-four-year history, he exhibits a humble spirit because of his difficult beginnings.

Last year, the twenty-one-year-old Williams went back to San Diego to be grand marshal of his high school's homecoming parade. The school wanted Williams to wear a tuxedo and ride in a convertible. He declined. "It would focus too much attention on me," he said.

"He's so friendly to everybody," Texas receiver Wayne McGarity told people. "You sit there and talk to him, and you think, 'Why aren't you cocky? Do you know who you are?'"

The friendliness comes from his upbringing, Williams says. "I'm nice because when I was growing up so many people weren't nice to me, and I remember how that felt. I don't want to make anyone else feel like that."

His parents divorced when Williams and his twin sister were five years old. That left Williams' mother, Sandy, to raise three children by herself. A purchasing agent who went to school at night, Sandy Williams put Ricky in charge of the house while she was away. He would take responsibility for putting his sisters to bed, doing the wash, and answering the phone only after a special signal that it was his mother calling.

Times were tough, but the Williams family stayed close. When Ricky signed a minor league baseball contract, he used his bonus to pay for his sisters' college tuition and move his mother to Austin. When his playing career is over, Williams wants to use his education degree from Texas to become an elementary school teacher.[6]

Life was not fair to John D. Rockefeller, either. John D's father was a con man. He would leave his family for months at a time, plying his trade of patent medicines and seducing young women. His mother, Eliza, was a prim, devout Baptist. Before the father left town, he would tell the local grocer to give his family what they needed, and he'd pay for it when he got back. Never knowing when this credit might be canceled, Eliza became extremely frugal and drilled her children in thrifty maxims such as "Willful waste makes woeful want."

Eliza taught John thrift, economy, and order. From his mother he also got a great devotion to God and the church. Rockefeller entered the oil business in the 1860s, when oil was being refined for kerosene. But of every barrel of oil distilled, only half was converted into the valuable fuel. Refiners would just dump whatever was left over. That appalled Rockefeller.

He honestly believed that if God put all of that stuff into the oil, there must be a use for it. He just had to find out what it was. He did. Soon after Rockefeller got his refineries up and running, he created one of the industry's first research and development departments. That department discovered how to turn oil byproducts into useful goods such as paraffin wax for candles, lubricating oils for machinery, and gasoline for fuel. What others were throwing away, Rockefeller was turning into profit. All because he had faith in God's wisdom.[7]

Learning Confidence from Unfairness

We want our children to take the seeming unfairness of life and turn it into a lifetime advantage of confidence. How do we encourage our children to confidently live in a world that has not been fair, is not fair now, and will never be fair?

1. Parents need to *acknowledge the unfairness* our child is experiencing, not deny it or make light of it. Our children need to know that we understand the pain of being hurt, offended, overlooked, or rejected, because we have "been there." It is helpful for the child if the parent can share a life experience, or a story from Scripture, or a book that relates to the particular unfairness that the child is experiencing.

A fifth grader explains it this way. "I like it when things are not fair, and my mom and I talk about it, and sometimes she even shares stories about similar stuff that happened when she was a little girl. That kind of builds my confidence because she helps me get through it."

2. Parents must *avoid overreacting*. There are times when the unfairness to a child triggers painful memories and times in the parent's life. Perhaps there are wounds from the past that are not healed or continuing problems in the life of the parent. When we see our child suffering in a similar situation, the flood of emotion causes us to do everything in our power to rescue the child and "make it right." In the majority of situations, we cannot and should not do this. The wise parent will recognize where the emotional tidal wave is coming from in their own life and use the unfairness to build confidence in both parent and child.

A fourth grader expresses heartfelt frustration. "My mom goes crazy when something bad happens to me. She screams at whoever did it to me. She screams at the teachers when I don't get the grade she thinks I should have. She's a real screamer. She takes away my confidence when she acts like that. I wish she wouldn't do those things. I wish she'd just back off."

3. *Allow time for healing*. Do not "Pollyana-ize" the situation during the crisis. No child wants to be told, "It's all for the best" or "It will make a man out of you" or "Don't worry about it. This happens to everyone." Depending on the severity of the unfairness, those kinds of truisms can be shared in the days, weeks, and months that follow as healing takes place.

"It takes away my confidence," a sixth grader shares, "when I'm hurting inside and my mom or dad just smiles and says, 'It will feel better tomorrow.' Sometimes it doesn't. I know."

4. Parents need to *model forgiveness*. It is extremely helpful for the child if the parent, although totally em-

pathetic to the unfairness the child is experiencing, encourages the child to forgive. The parent and child can walk through the forgiveness stages together. "From our research and experience, one truth predominates: The art of forgiveness is the secret of a contented life," Foster Cline, M.D., a psychiatrist, said. "Good mental health depends on living in a constant state of forgiveness."

"There is freedom in forgiveness. Freedom, stability, and self-control in life always accompany forgiveness."[8] Forgiveness is a powerful tool for building confidence. A child whose parent encourages forgiveness, rather than nursing the grudges of unfairness, is giving a gift of resiliency to the child that will build confidence to deal with the future assaults of unfairness. A sixth grader recalls, "Once my mom was really mad at my teacher and thought she had been really unfair to me. She even yelled at the teacher to her face and called her all kinds of names behind her back. That made me feel very unconfident. Later on, my mom apologized to me about it, and forgave the teacher, and told the teacher so. I was very proud of my mom for being big enough to forgive. I think her confidence is growing. I know what she did helped my confidence."

Scripture encourages us to "Be gentle and ready to forgive; never hold grudges. Remember, the Lord forgave you, so you must forgive others" (Col. 3:13, TLB).

5. Parents need to *encourage a child to be patient,* to keep on trying, and to not give up in spite of the inevitable trials and discouragements. Both the parent and child will be tempted with the "throw in the towel," "take my toys and go home" mentality. Charles Colson said it well. "God calls me to be faithful, not successful. The end result is in His hands, not mine." Scripture encourages parent and child. "Patience develops strength of character in us and helps us trust

God more each time we use it until finally our hope and faith are strong and steady" (Rom. 5:4, TLB).

A third grader sweetly reports, "I like it when my mom and dad pray with me and pray that I won't give up even when my feelings are hurt or something bad has happened."

Susan B. Anthony was relentless as she blazed the path for women to obtain the right to vote. In spite of the long years of rebuffs and snide remarks, she tirelessly continued. At the end of her life, she urged one of her successors, "Take your stand and hold it. Let come what will. Receive blows like a good soldier." She stands as an example of applied confidence.

6. Parents need to help their children *develop an attitude of gratitude* that chooses to focus on what they have, rather than what they have lost, or been deprived of, because of unfairness.

A fifth grader gives proper perspective. "I think my parents help me with confidence by telling me about all the stuff I have to be thankful for, and they tell me not to feel bad when I lose, or am not even chosen, or even worse, when I'm ignored. But it's still hard sometimes." Of course it is. But this child's parents are providing an important confidence tool that will serve the child well through all of life.

7. We need to *give children continual encouragement.* They, like us, need to realize that the trials of unfairness that come their way are not enemies of faith but are opportunities to prove God's faithfulness. Sharing stories from Scripture and from the lives of family and friends is a powerful way for their God-confidence to take root and grow.

A fifth grader asserts, "A parent should talk to the child and try to understand their feelings. Example: If a child comes home feeling bad because another child has made fun of the way they look or did something, a parent should tell the child that God does not care how we look or how we do things but it is what is inside that counts."

8. Parents and children need to *pour out our hearts of hurt and frustration* to the Lord. It is therapeutic for a child to see the tears of a parent and hear the cries of a parent who does not understand "why this had to happen" to the child but is still choosing to accept it and cling to the Lord in prayer. Bonds of trust and confidence come as a parent and child plead with God in prayer together. Mother Teresa realized that "prayer is the mortar that holds our house together."

A fourth grader shares: "Some of my most favorite times are when mom and dad pray for me before bed-time when I'm going through my hard times at school or in sports. It builds my confidence better than any-thing."

The words of this song are comforting to a parent and a child who is dealing with one of the many, many unfair situations of life:

> God is too wise to be mistaken.
> God is too good to be unkind.
> So when you don't understand,
> When you don't see His plan,
> When you can't trace His hand,
> Trust His Heart.[9]

5

"My Child Has Rights"

"Confidence is trusting God to do something or prevent something as well as believing in God to help you do something accurately."
—*Third grader*

There is a four-letter word that no parent wants to hear. Yet almost every year the dreaded word circulates in the world of parents and children—LICE!

This particular year, a responsible parent reported that her child had contracted lice and had been treated. Nevertheless, the school sent out the standard lice notice indicating that there had been an outbreak and listing symptoms, cures, and precautions.

The following day, a mother of a fourth grader informed the teacher that she suspected that the girl sitting next to her son had lice, wanted the girl checked and her son's seat moved immediately.

The fourth-grade teacher reminded the mother that the notice had been sent and that she did not think it was necessary to either check the girl or change her son's seat. The mother was not happy.

After school, the irate mother came to the front office with an equally disgruntled friend. They informed the office that this boy's rights were being violated. They said that the law stated that the school was required to check the "suspicious" girl for the sake of protecting the health rights of the boy. (An interpretation of California law that was not accurate.) The school verified the law regarding the rights of both the son and the suspected carrier of lice, and notified the mother.

The next morning, the extremely angry and agitated mother demanded to speak with me. The office staff told her I was in a meeting but could schedule an appointment. She could not wait. "My son's rights are being violated!" She tried to get through the office by force. The staff prevented her, so she pushed her way through a back entrance and stormed through my closed office door, interrupting the meeting because of her presumed emergency.

The matters of the mother violating the rights of school personnel, school property, and school students were handled in order. The suspected girl did not, indeed, have lice, nor had she ever contracted lice.

Whose Rights?

In my son's preparatory school there was one rule: Your rights end where the next person's begin! It's easy to say, simple to remember, and makes perfect common sense. The difficulties of interpretation cause the sticky problems.

Recently two Florida high school football players and their parents challenged a school disciplinary policy that suspends from extracurricular activities any students involved in drinking. The boys were caught drinking and were suspended from the team for thirty days. The parents complained that the policy is unconstitutional and violates their right to privacy.

Because of the parents' uproar, the boys' suspension has been tabled, pending legal clarification of the disciplinary policy. The boys have not missed a game. A court will have to determine whether the school's policy is constitutional or whether it violates the boys' rights.

Unfortunately, in much of society today, the interpretation of *rights* for our children has become confused with "entitlements." "It's my right!" has come to mean, "I'm entitled to it!" This is another way of saying, "I deserve whatever it is, when I want it, and I don't have to work for it or wait for it 'cause I'm me! I have more rights than other people!"

This reasoning is both selfish and fallacious. My wise friend, Pat Mac, often says, "Parents today are raising The Entitlement Generation. Children grow up believing they are owed privileges they have not earned."

The overempowerment of children under the guise of protecting their presumed rights or showing them due respect is not a positive change for children or for society. Too many of our children are being taught, "When in doubt, it must be someone else's fault." We can see this assumption in action everywhere:

- In academics: "My child didn't get a good grade. It's the teacher's fault."

- In sports: "My child wasn't the star. It's the coaches' fault."

- In friendships: "My child hit him. What did he do to provoke my child?"

- In social situations: "That can't be true. My child never says things like that."

Richard Carlson, Ph.D., and author of *Don't Sweat the Small Stuff. . . It's All Small Stuff,* says, "This type of blaming has become extremely common in our culture. On a personal level, it has led us to believe that we are never completely responsible for our own actions, problems, or happiness. On a societal level, it has led to frivolous lawsuits and ridiculous excuses that get criminals off the hook. When we are in the habit of blaming others, we will blame others for our anger, frustration, depression, stress, and unhappiness."[10]

Bjorn Borg has the reputation of being the toughest two-hander tennis champion ever to play the game. He won the Wimbledon Tournament five times and the French Open six times.

> Unlike some other players, Borg never wasted his energy by getting emotional, throwing rackets or smashing his fists into the clay. Instead, he preferred to be like the eye of a storm, calmly and confidently watching his competitors' outbursts.
>
> It wasn't always that way. In fact, as a child, he could be a sore loser. When Borg flubbed at a local tennis tournament in his hometown of Sodertalje, Sweden, he threw a tantrum on the court, yelling and throwing his racket.
>
> His father, disgusted with Borg's unsportsmanlike behavior, met him at the side of the tennis court and promptly took his racket away. Borg immediately realized that in order to play he would have to behave like a gentleman.[11]

Children are resilient and moldable, especially at the early ages. One of the greatest satisfactions parents and teachers enjoy is encouraging children to develop positive character qualities that will mold their future lives for good and not for evil, for confidence and not for failure. Six crucial character qualities to focus on developing during the years of childhood are these: kindness, obedience, honesty, respect (for authority, for property, for others, and for themselves), responsibility, and self-control.

In the school where I am administrator, sometimes we think we have heard every possible story a parent or child might have to tell. In spite of this, we never cease to grieve when parents wrongly defend their children and deprive them of character-building opportunities. In like manner, we rejoice greatly when parents encourage their children with the building blocks of character development.

Recently we hired a girls' coach and a boys' coach who had each attended the school during their childhoods. Growing up, Kelly was a delight and is just as charming and capable as an adult. Nick had some problems with self-control in the classroom and on the playing field. He was competitive, sometimes impulsive, and occasionally explosive. The combination led to several trips to my office.

With each trip, the routine was the same. I read the paperwork. Then asked Nick, "Why are you here?" Each time he gave the facts without defensiveness. Then I showed him the paperwork and asked if the situation was represented accurately. He would read and sadly nod his head. "Yup! That's what happened all right." (Let me hasten to add, that if and when any child ever disagrees with the paperwork, the authority figure who wrote up the child is brought in to discuss the matter with the child and with me. This is done out of respect for the child as well as the authority figure—teacher, coach, lunch staff, before/after school staff, etc. None of us is infallible. The point of correction is to build men and women of character, not engage in foolish power struggles!)

Then Nick needed to be forgiven by the person wronged, by the authority figure, and most importantly by God for his mistake. I remember one time hearing Nick's prayer: "Dear God, I'm sorry I did [whatever]. I just wasn't thinking, and then I did it! Thank you for loving me even when I do wrong things. Please forgive me 'cause I'm really sorry. I don't want to do it again. Please help me to be kind and obedient and respectful and responsible and self-controlled from now on. Thank you."

Nick's willingness to assume responsibility for his mistakes and accept the consequences was honoring to his parents and gave a glimpse into the man that he has become and that the school was pleased to hire.

Of course children will make mistakes—lots and lots of them. So what if they do? Naturally we expect them. But rather than defending, rationalizing, blaming, or excusing the behavior, why not use it as a character-building opportunity? Having the child admit the wrongdoing, get forgiveness, accept the consequence, and carry on is the simple recipe for dealing with the common mistakes of childhood if parents want to build men or women of confident character. Please take every opportunity to notice that a truly confident adult is able to admit making a mistake, is able to ask for forgiveness, is able to accept the consequence and to keep on going!

God-Given Rights

Being created in the image of God certainly gives both parents and children some inalienable rights. God gives unconditional love. We can do nothing to earn more love from God. We can do nothing to take away his unconditional love. God gives us forgiveness of sins when we ask and are truly repentant. Of course, God does not take away the earthly consequences of our sin but is always there to help us as we live with the consequences of our unfortunate choices. God gives us the security of his presence in this life and hope of heaven for the next.

Unconditional love, forgiveness, and security are "rights" that God freely gives. Man does not. Because parents are human, we struggle with our imperfections as we strive to give love, forgiveness, and security to our children. Our human tendency is to lose balance. Sometimes parents smother love. Other parents ignore their children. Still other parents may emotionally abuse children with screaming and hurting words. There are also those parents who abuse children physically or sexually. Parents are known to ignore wrong behavior in children or become inappropriately harsh. Sometimes the consequences parents select do not fit the wrongdoing or the child. Other times parents do not really forgive but bring up past incidents over and over again. Although parents want to give security to their children, the lack of stability in their own lives is passed on to the kids.

Isn't it interesting to notice that even Almighty God does not give rights that are devoid of personal responsibility on the part of the receiver? God does love unconditionally. However, comprehending the love of God requires that the individual get to know God, and the better the person knows God, the more the person has the capability of understanding the unconditional love. The same is true of God's gift of forgiveness. Before an individual can be forgiven, the person must acknowledge that there is something that needs to be forgiven, accept responsibility for the wrongdoing, and humbly ask for forgiveness with a repentant spirit. God grants the security of his presence in this life and in the next, but only the one who seeks to know him can begin to appropriate this security.

What is true for God in dealing with us, I believe is true in our dealing with our children. Rights that are given without the balance of responsibilities have a great potential for abuse.

When a parent accepts the "right" to be the undisputed authority figure, and takes no responsibility for acknowledging and administering the rights of the child, an abusive situation results. When a child is given the "right" to control the family without respecting the other family members, the parents can become victims of manipulation.

What are some of the rights a child has? What are the corresponding responsibilities? The following is a partial list of a child's rights and responsibilities.

→ A child has the right to be treated with dignity and respect. The child has the responsibility to treat others with the same dignity and respect that he/she desires.

→ A child has the right to express feelings. The child has the responsibility to respect the feelings of others and listen to the expression of feelings from others.

→ A child has the right to express needs and wants. A child has the responsibility to balance those needs and wants with the needs and wants of others.

→ A child has the right to make mistakes, to learn from them, to change and to grow. A child has the responsibility to give others the same opportunities.

→ A child has the right to develop his/her own uniqueness and not be compared with others or pushed into a certain mold. A child has the responsibility to allow others to be unique and different from himself or herself.

→ A child has the right to know God. A child has the responsibility to love, honor, and obey God.

All other specific rights and privileges grow out of this basic set of rights. In discussing this listing with a highly respected California therapist, Madelon Dribble, LCSW, MFCC, she defined responsibility as "A good ability to respond appropriately to things." The all encompassing responsibility of rights is expressed succinctly in the "golden rule" of Matthew 7:12 and Luke 6:31: Do to others as you would have them do to you.

One of the most difficult things in life is to sacrifice or give up personal rights for the benefit of another. Only a supremely mature and confident person will have the ability to make such a sacrifice without feelings of resentment and loss. Yet every mature adult knows that being a friend, a spouse, an adult child of aging parents, and/or a parent involves the continual making of small and large sacrifices on a regular basis.

Children first learn about relinquishing rights from their parents. Of course, Jesus is the supreme example of the sacrifice of rights. We are told in Philippians 2:8 that the only Son of God left his throne in heaven, "humbled himself and became obedient to the point of death, even the death of the cross" (NKJV).

I believe that a child can be better equipped for the inevitable hills of difficulty and valleys of humiliation in life by learning in childhood to graciously relinquish rights rather than to endlessly fight for them. Many parents are engaged in legitimate battles to obtain legitimate rights for their children. Is the struggle worth their time, their strength, their financial and emotional resources? Sometimes, yes. Other times, no.

Asking such questions as, "Will it matter next year?" or "Will it make a difference ten years from now?" will give clues as to the significance of the specific issue in the scheme of life. Perhaps the confidence of the child will be better developed by giving up the right rather than fighting for it. A sixth grader expressed it this way: "Sometimes I feel my confidence is weakened when my mom and dad scream at the coaches about stuff that really doesn't matter. Even though it hurts, it's okay with me when I sit on the bench most of the game to let the better players play. I know they are better than me. I know they can help the team win better than I can. Besides, those guys are my friends. I'm rooting for them. I wish my parents would just stay out of it."

The development of confident character is almost always, "Two steps forward, and one step back." Parents must have a mindset that sees their mistakes and the mistakes of their children as necessary tools for growth. This thought, based on Galatians 5:22 and 23, may help to keep the big picture in mind. I have shared it with many parents. Some have even put it on their refrigerators as a daily reminder:

Love is the expression of God-confidence
Joy is the strength of God-confidence
Peace is the security of God-confidence
Patience is the endurance of God-confidence
Kindness is the conduct of God-confidence
Goodness is the character of God-confidence
Faithfulness is the persistence of God-confidence
Gentleness is the humility of God-confidence
Self-control is the victory of God-confidence

6

"I Should Be My Child's Best Friend"

"Confidence is not being scared of something and trusting in the Lord to do it. An example is David in the Bible. He fought and killed Goliath."
—Third grader

The couple had tried unsuccessfully for years to have a child. There had been multiple pregnancies, but each had resulted in an early miscarriage. After fifteen years of yearning, the perfect little girl was born. This "miracle baby" was the answer to countless prayers and tears of anguish through the night.

When the time for school began, the enthusiastic mother volunteered to be a part of everything involving her daughter. In fact, the mother spent all day every day being a part of the school, church, and neighborhood activities that included her daughter. The father also scheduled his work time so that he could be an active participant.

In second grade, the teacher spoke to the mother about an incident where the girl used inappropriate language. The mother said, "I know every word my child knows. My child does not know that word and would never say it."

At a parent conference in third grade, the mother proudly announced, "My daughter is my best friend. We do everything together, and she tells me everything." She also had the daughter's hair cut to resemble her own hair style. At about this time, the mother and father began having marital problems.

In fourth grade, the daughter was having some difficulty getting along with another girl. The mother vehemently denied any wrongdoing on her daughter's part and greeted her daughter at the close of each school day with, "So what did that nasty girl say to you today?"

In fifth and sixth grade, the mother began to dress more like the daughter, and continued to refer to her daughter as "my best friend." She excitedly reported to the other mothers that she and her daughter could now "trade clothes and shoes." She would continue to deny any reports of wrongdoing on her daughter's part with the rationale, "I know everything about my daughter. She is my best friend. She would never do that or say that. I know."

Keeping Roles Clear

Through the years, I have observed that it is not unusual for an older mother of an only child to become overinvolved emotionally in the life of her child, sometimes even to the detriment of the marital relationship. In this example, the daughter actively rebelled against the mother in the junior and senior high years. Ultimately, the mother lost her daughter and "best friend," as well as doing irreparable damage to her relationship with her husband.

A parent who wishes to be the child's best friend ends up following the child rather than leading the way. There are mothers of teenagers who compromise standards to attend or participate in questionable events with their teens. The mothers suspend their value systems in order to hang on to the best friend illusion for as long as possible.

It is tempting for a loving mother to want to be her child's best friend. I can clearly recall the following incident, although it happened years ago. I went to pick up my son from the three-year-old department at church. The teacher came to me with an amused look on her face. "We were teaching the children the song, 'Jesus is my best friend.' Your son insisted, 'No he isn't. My mommy is my best friend.'" I tried to talk with him, but he was not convinced. 'Jesus is not my best friend. My mommy is.'" To tell the truth, I was elated! To this day, I think that it is a sweet and innocent endearment from a young child.

The danger comes, however, when perspective and balance are blurred or lost. Dr. Laura Schlessinger and Rabbi Stewart Vogel use strong words:

> Instead of guidelines and moral modeling, we live in a society in which many parents abdicate their important responsibility to parent and sometimes treat their children like royalty, endowing them with papal infallibility. Children are believed before other adults and even teachers because "of course, my child would never lie." Acknowledging that the child really did "do bad" would be to face their own inadequate parenting, availability, commitment, and circumstances. Additionally, the "me generation" folks often only see their children as extensions of their own egos and defend against any assault on their self-esteem.[12]

The words of Deuteronomy 6:7 clearly state the daily practical guidelines of parental responsibility. "Impress them [the Commandments] on your children. Talk about them when you sit at home and when you walk along the road, when you lie down and when you get up."

The following questions might be helpful in keeping the balance between being a parent and being a friend.

1. Is your child being mothered or smothered? Do you have a life that is separate from your child, or do you depend on your child for your sense of fulfillment, your reason for being? No child can handle the stress of being all things to a parent. A parent who becomes overly involved in the child's world in order to deny, block out, or postpone dealing with unpleasant issues or relationships of their own life is guaranteed to cause unnecessary future pain for both the child and himself or herself.

A sixth grader discloses, "Since my mom and dad got divorced, my mom spends all of her time hovering around me. I like her around, but she is overdoing it. I know she is lonely but I wish she had another life. I think I'm her whole life. That makes me nervous, and steals some of my confidence."

2. Are you realistic about the strengths and weaknesses of your child? Or is your own sense of personhood so fragile that your child must be perfect so that you will appear stronger and more accomplished? Children need to know that they are accepted just as they are, with all their strengths and weaknesses. Healthy individuals are able to realize that they have both strengths and weaknesses. They accept those strengths and weaknesses, and are capable of genuinely rejoicing in the successes of others.

This fifth grader gives perspective: "A parent should always encourage and compliment a child, but not too much, which would make them proud. Example: If a mom says a child is doing something good on homework, and later the child does something wrong, the mom should not be afraid to discipline properly. Correct discipline will not break down a child's confidence."

A fourth grader suggests," A parent should give the children compliments when they do well on something, but when they aren't working to their full potential, encourage them to do better. Example: You did a nice job, but next time try to work a little harder."

3. Do you spend time doing fun things with your child that your child is interested in doing with you? Or do you insist on controlling the situations for your own purposes? "I have fun with my mom," this fourth grader relates. "She gives me a choice of two or three things to do, and we do the thing together. Some kids don't get to choose. Their mom does all the choosing. That wouldn't be as much fun. I know my mom helps to build my confidence."

Likewise, do you spend time away from your children doing things with friends? If you don't have a life outside of your family, then you will have trouble maintaining an appropriate role with your children.

4. Do you encourage your children to make friendships within their peer groups? You should not be your child's only friend. Your child needs playmates his or her own age. However, you can play a role in the choices your child makes. A parent can strongly influence a child's ability to make and to keep good friends. A fifth grader gives this example: "I can always tell when my mom likes my friend. She lets me go places with the friend and the friend's family. If she didn't like the person, that would never happen."

5. Do your children know that they can count on you for wise counsel, not just for blind defense? Maturing children need to be able to pour out their hurt and frustration to parents, knowing that the parents will lovingly sift through the children's pain and use the experience to help the children grow stronger and wiser, emotionally and spiritually.

"I know I can always go to my parents when bad

things happen," a sixth grader shares. "They will listen
and give me advice on what they think and give me
advice about what to do next time. Even when they
don't agree with what I did, or think I was right, they
still help me to think things through and to learn from
the experience. I really appreciate that. We also pray
together and ask God for wisdom."

Children need parents who can be a type of friend
who does not sacrifice parental wisdom, counsel, and
good judgment.

7

"I Owe My Child the Best of Everything!"

"Confidence is when you know you can do something or when you're determined to do something!"
—Third grader

The league game to decide which team would be in the play-offs had begun! Everyone was excited. We had a particularly strong baseball team and had high expectations. The scheduling of the game had been difficult this year because of weather conditions and tie-breaking games. The families were aware of these possible problems before the season began but were still given a week's notice regarding this all-important game.

Tension mounted as the game was tied at the top of the fifth inning. Then it happened. Three of our top hitters had to leave. They had a Little League game. It would take thirty minutes to get there. The coach was irate. "You can't be committed to two games on the same day at the same time in two different leagues!" The parents shrugged. That's the way it was. The players and parents hopped into their respective Suburban, SUV, and van. The caravan drove off, leaving a stunned coach and a disheartened, fragmented team.

Our team lost the game, the opportunity to go to the play-offs, and the possibility of winning the league championship.

The parents of the three Little League players had an idea. "Let's replay the game, since our guys had to leave." Needless to say, the coaches and athletic directors of the league were totally unreceptive to that suggestion. The parents persisted. One father approached me. "You need to stand up for our kids. Our team could have made it to the play-offs and won the championship! See what you can do."

I discovered that the Little League game had been lost, and so our league was the "only opportunity left for a big win." I also discovered that our coach and athletic director knew the boys were also in Little League and made as many allowances for them as possible, but had no control over the scheduling of this critical game. Nothing could be changed. Choices were made. Consequences followed.

Sports Overkill?

It is not particularly unusual today for a child to be in two different leagues during the same season of the same sport. I asked a few moms what it's like for them. "I hate it," one of the moms blurted out. "I have no life. I live to drive from one game to the next. I don't even need a home during the baseball season. We are never there. There are games all weekend every weekend. During the week, there are practices and more games. During vacation times, there are an endless number of games and play-offs. It never ends. I wish my son had never played baseball."

Then she began to talk about the rude and crude behavior of the parents and the coaches who would do anything to win. "You have no idea," she exploded. "In order to get their boys on the best team in the league, some of these parents use phony addresses. They think nothing of schmoozing the coaches to get their kids to be able to play certain positions. The coaches not only let it happen, they encourage it! This sport also brings out the worst in these win-at-any-cost parents. They are brutally competitive. And the yelling and cursing of the parents at the games is terrible. Some of them act like animals! It makes me ashamed to be a part of the human race. I'm learning to hate baseball and all it represents."

I wondered if she would allow her son to continue playing in the two leagues next season. She sighed deeply and spoke with a quiet tone of regretful acceptance. "Oh, I guess so. It means a lot to him."

Baseball is an American tradition. Both Dad and Grandpa played Little League. The classic song "Take Me Out to the Ball Game" joyfully expresses the enthusiasm and zest Americans have for the great American pastime. What has happened to that carefree attitude? Where did the sheer fun of playing the game go?

Leigh Steinberg is a powerful sports attorney and agent. He routinely makes astounding financial deals for elite athletes. His comments from his book *Winning with Integrity* are profound:

> The professional athletes of today live, more than ever before, in a world of external adulation, to the extent that many of them do not generally build strong internal values. Too many of them are self-absorbed, convinced that they are the center of the world and that everyone else is there to serve them. Too many of them wind up disconnected from the rest of society, and that is dangerous in many ways.
>
> I have watched this disconnection of athletes from society become increasingly pronounced in the past quarter century. By and large, the players I see today have not grown up with the same sense of idealism that their predecessors did. They

think of sports much more as a business than as a game. From the time they first begin drawing attention for their talent—for some of them, before they are even in high school—that talent is equated with the riches and fame of professional sports. Early on, for many of these young athletes, the game becomes a means to an end as much as an end in itself. And their sense of competitiveness extends much further than the boundaries of the playing field.[13]

I firmly believe that the driving force behind much of the imbalance now seen in grade-school sports is parental competitiveness and the dream of ultimate financial rewards. The problems begin early.

The Competitive Edge

Several years ago, a father wanted to enroll his five year old in our school but wanted to make certain the boy did not go into kindergarten until he was at least six. Knowing the family and the maturation level of the child, I did not understand the peculiar request. "My son is already outstanding in T-ball. He's the best on the team. The coach sees a future in baseball ahead for him. I want to give my son the best of everything, but know I can't afford it. If he can achieve in sports, he's got it made. So I figure the longer I can keep him in school, the better chance he has of getting an athletic scholarship to a really great college or university." I have since discovered that same thinking in parents hoping for academic success for their children as well.

How are the children reacting? Sure, they want to be the next superstar. Why not? What little child has not seen his or her favorite athletic celebrity's face plastered on TV, billboards, magazines, etc., advertising the shoe to wear, the food to eat, the drink that gives the boost. That same child hears parents talking about the fantastic fortunes these heroes are making. The children buy into the parents' dream of glory and riches with every cell in their hopeful bodies.

The fantasy is easy. The reality of being in the game is tough. Trying to meet the unrealistic expectations of parents is often hurtful for the children and is a primary cause of stress. Many children in my study voice similar concerns about parents damaging their confidence level during sports.

"A parent should not put pressure on a child," reports one sensitive sixth grader. "This will cause the child to get stressed out. If the child fails they'll feel terrible. I know. That's what happened to me in baseball last year. Because I got out with bases loaded, the team lost. My father and mother were yelling and screaming when I was at the plate. I couldn't even think I was so nervous. I still feel terrible about it. I don't know if I want to try out for the team next year. Jesus said, 'My burden is light.'"

Another sixth grader agrees: "Parents should never put their child down. They should never ever say things bad that would make the child stop being determined. Instead of saying what we're not good at, parents should say what we are good at, like encouraging us after a bad game instead of going over and over what we did wrong."

Parents can stifle self-esteem: "It kills my confidence when my parents go on and on about my mistakes in sports. They keep mentioning the subject over the years. I don't like it," a fifth grader reports. Likewise, parents can kill confidence when they make kids do things they're not good at. "Parents should encourage their child in things he or she is good at. Example: If your child's interest is in music, don't push them to play baseball, soccer, basketball, etc. It's bad for their confidence," says another fifth grader.

Marta Conley, Athletic Director at our school, has deep and abiding love for children. She shares this poem that was originally printed in the *Cullman* (Alabama) *Times*. Although the original paper is old and yellowed, the emotion evoked is fresh and heart wrenching.

He's Just a Little Boy

He stands at the plate with his heart pounding
    fast;
The bases are loaded; the die has been cast.
Mom and dad cannot help him; he stands all
    alone.
A hit at this moment would send the team home.

The ball nears the plate; he swings and he misses.
There's a groan from the crowd, with some boos
    and hisses.
A thoughtless voice cries, "Strike out the bum!"
Tears fill his eyes; the game's no longer fun.

Remember—he's just a little boy who stands all
    alone.
So open your heart and give him a break,
For it's moments like this a man you can make.
Keep this in mind when you hear someone forget.
He's just a little boy, not a man yet.

Today's loving and conscientious parents want to "be there" for their children. I have noticed the growing presence of dads who take time off to attend games, programs, and other special school events. Stay-at-home moms commit to a large block of time in volunteer work at school and at church. Moms with part-time or full-time employment strive to take time off work to be a part of the programs and activities that are scheduled on the yearly calendar. No parent wants to bear the guilt of hearing the piercing words, "You weren't there for me."

Sometimes it seems to me that there is an unspoken competition between parents to see who can win the "be, do, and give everything" to their children prize. I have observed the stressed faces of exhausted parents who consistently try too hard to do too much too often. I have sensed that the pressure is coming from within themselves, and not from their children.

Joel Norris, Ph.D., is an outspoken professor of Atmospheric Science at the University of California at Irvine. "I think family has become one of the prime idols of conservative evangelicals. Sacrificing for family sounds holy, but my own experience as a child suggests there is often more selfishness in it than meets the eye."

Certainly God requires us to provide for our children, but does that mean we fail as parents if we do not provide weekly soccer, music lessons, and art classes? We hustle out of church and spend the afternoon and all waking hours the rest of the week whisking our kids from event to event. Parents act as if they must suck the marrow out of childhood for fear that it will pass too quickly and their children will arrive at adulthood not having achieved their full athletic, social, musical, and artistic potential. Give me a kid who knows how to mow the lawn, participate in a conversation around the family dinner table, serve an elderly neighbor, and participate in devotional time with the family!

By becoming inordinately concerned with the "personal growth" of our children, do we not neglect the weightier matters?

Parents as well as children are feeling stressed by the frenetic pace and the frenzied race to be involved in a plethora of activities. Trapped in this whirlwind of Go and Do, parents and children alike have no time to relax, to contemplate, to think. In talking with hundreds of children each week, one thing comes up again and again. "I wish I had some free time. I'm always having to go somewhere and do something." Children and parents are overcommitted and overscheduled. There are an excessive number of choices available to children, and parents become trapped by their desires to provide "the best of everything" for them.

Truly the Best

The unfortunate thing is that these parents are not, indeed, giving their children the best. What is, in fact, the best? Psychiatrist Ronald Dahl of the Pittsburgh Medical Center expresses concern about what our kids are experiencing. "Surrounded by ever-greater stimulation, their young faces look disappointed and bored. I'm concerned about the cumulative effect of years at these levels of feverish activity. It is no mystery to me why many teenagers appear apathetic and burned out, with a 'been there, done that' air of indifference toward much of life."[14]

How can we avoid burning out our kids? We can help them to recognize what is really important. Several months ago I was speaking at a chapel for first and second graders. I was asking them how their parents encouraged them to get to know God. Many hands were raised. The children knew. They mentioned things like going to church together, going to a Christian school, memorizing Bible verses, and having family times of Bible stories and prayer together.

A second-grade girl's hand continued to wave in the air. Knowing the family situation, I eagerly called on her. "I spend five minutes in the morning before school reading a Bible story in my room by myself and having my own prayer time."

I asked, "Has this helped you in any way?"

"Oh yes," she responded with confidence and enthusiasm. "It has helped me to get to know God in a way that I feel close to him even when my parents aren't around. I ask God to help me to control myself. It's working, isn't it, Mrs. Holt? Aren't I a lot better this year?"

Oh yes! This bright girl had been having so many problems with self-control in first grade that her parents and I weren't sure she was going to be able to continue in our school. I loved the parents. They had many struggles to overcome, including divorce, drugs, remarriage, and employment uncertainties. They had no positive role modeling from their own parents. They are building a new life day by day with God's help, and they know it. This confident second grader was able to recognize that spending time alone with God is a vital component of her emotional and spiritual maturation.

The Small Things

Parents often deceive themselves into thinking that giving their child "the best of everything" has to do with lavish expenditures or indulgent hyperactivity. A sixth grader gives a simple, sweet idea that is available to every parent. "An example of a way to build someone up is to write little notes and hide them in their lunches or under their pillows or inside their books. Write on the note how special they are and tell them about what good things they do. That will build their confidence every time."

Another way to build up kids is to help them develop an attitude of gratitude. A fourth grader sets the tone:

> We take our lives for granted. We think of how there are people better off than us instead of those

worse off than us. People say, "There is no God because I don't have a mansion," while they drive past a man living on the street. If anybody does that, they should remember the saying, "I cried because I had no shoes until I met a man who had no feet." Though I have had quite a few hardships in my life, and I sometimes complain, I do have many things to be thankful for. I have my friends and family who love and support me, a roof over my head, food to nourish my body, the ability to think, walk, and talk. Most of all I'm thankful for Christ dying on the cross for my sins and your sins. This Thanksgiving and everyday, thank God for what you've got.

Shortly before this was written, the child's divorced parents were screaming at each other in the school parking lot while angrily pulling the child from one to the other. The police were called to settle the dispute. The angry custody battle continues. So does the child's thankful heart and unwavering trust in God.

To help children focus on being thankful, families utilize different ideas. Some families create "gratitude diaries." At the end of each month, they make a list of what each member of the family is grateful for from that month and record it in a family diary of gratitude. Periodically, the family rereads the list from the previous month.

The "blessing box" is another familiar idea. Decorate a box or container. Then, whenever the Lord gives a blessing or answers a prayer, the family member writes the blessing on a piece of paper and slips it inside the box. Monthly, the box is opened, and the slips of paper are taken out and read. Both of these simple ideas help parents and children to focus on appreciating what God has already given rather than fixating on what is lacking.

For every parent who wants to give their children what is truly the best of everything, there is an escape from the manic hyperactivity of excess required by our culture. But it takes the courage, confidence, and commitment of the parent. The following checklist will help parents evaluate if they are leading the next generation into character and confidence.

Am I teaching my children:

To know God in a personal way
To memorize Scripture
To value time alone
To be gracious and humble
To be responsible
To not blame others for their mistakes
That life is not fair
That money is a limited commodity
To negotiate
To be kind to others because it is the right thing
    to do
To be forgiving
That not everyone will like them no matter what
    they do or do not do
That they are not an exception to established
    rules and regulations
That character does count!

If parents focus on endowing their children with this sort of spiritual inheritance, their children will develop into men or women of godly character and confidence.

8

"I Just Want Her to Be Happy and to Feel Good About Herself"

"I think that confidence is assurance in oneself. It is sort of like self-esteem. I often categorize people into followers and leaders. Followers are usually people with less confidence. That does not mean it is bad to be a follower, as long as you can think for yourself. If you don't have confidence, you are more likely to give in to peer pressure."
—Sixth grader

The older son had gone through our school, was a conscientious student, was well liked, and had done well. The younger son was the baby of the family. The mother assured us that this son was extremely bright but had to be handled more gently than the first son. Not wanting to make snap judgments, the staff observed the child, ready and willing to allow for individual differences.

It appeared to the teachers that this son was less motivated to work and, at times, expressed resistance to trying. He also had some difficulty making friendships because of his aggressive and demanding behaviors.

The mother began to complain about homework, saying, "It is just plain silly to ask a child who has been in school working all day to come home and do more work." The teacher pointed out that the work assigned was identical to the amount her elder son had, and there had never been a problem. "Well, the world has changed. What was right five years ago is wrong now. My son just isn't happy when he comes home. He doesn't want to do homework, and I don't think he should have to."

The unhappiness continued the following year. So did the complaints. Too much homework. Too many discouraging grades. "The children are picking on my boy." "He's not happy at school. What are you going to do about it?"

After a multitude of conferences during the next two years, it became obvious to the mother that the school was not going to change academic or behavorial standards to ensure her child's happiness. She found a different school the following year.

Every time I heard about the boy in the years that followed, he was in a different school. She kept searching for that one school that could "make him happy and make him feel good about himself."

When the boy was in tenth grade, I met the mother in a local grocery store. She was elated and could not wait to tell me the news. "I have found the perfect school. It's worth the drive—one hour each way. Let me tell you what they do. I'm certain you will want to do it, too. Every child in the school always gets an A." I asked her to explain. "Well, if the child does a paper that, for some reason, is not an A, he keeps doing it until he gets an A, but only the A grade is recorded. Isn't that revolutionary?" I agreed it was. "His self-esteem has never been higher," she cooed. "It's the first time in his life he has ever been able to earn A's."

Several years later I saw the mother again. She was obviously distressed. "I don't understand what's happening. My boy made some bad friends. He's had some trouble with drugs and with the law. I know he's a good boy, and that it is not his fault. All I want is for him to be happy and feel good about himself. That's all I've ever wanted."

Happiness Is a Choice

The mother in this story failed in her calculating attempts to make her son happy. By removing him from situations involving stress or challenge, she robbed him of the important character-building opportunities of childhood. If happiness is the goal for our children, two things are certain:

> → 1. We will not reach it. "Happiness can never be the goal. Happiness is a byproduct of character. In people who develop strong character, there is a dramatically higher level of happiness than in those who live to chase after the next good time."[15]

> → 2. We will cripple our children by cheating them of character-building opportunities all through their lives. Many of life's lessons that develop character can be taught most effectively if parents let children experience consequences without interference.

Once a science teacher sent his student into the woods to observe a cocoon. The student watched intently as the butterfly's wings began to break through the silken fibers. He watched and waited, then grew impatient. It was taking so long, and the butterfly was putting forth enormous effort with uncertain results. Unable to stand the seeming futility of the struggle any longer, the student reached in with a delicate finger and tenderly helped the butterfly out of the cocoon. Pleased with the result, he watched as the butterfly flew a few feet, then spiraled to the earth and died.

The student was aghast. What had happened? He hurried back to his teacher who explained, "When you reached in to help, you deprived the butterfly of the opportunity to strengthen its wings in the struggle that was essential for life."

Just as the butterfly had to struggle to gain strength for survival in the outside world, so our children must learn the difficult lessons of responsibility in order to be able to fly as mature adults. Rescuing our children, protecting them from becoming responsible, and preventing them from experiencing the consequences of their choices will result in crippled adults who will never fly with strength, confidence, and independence. A parent who has triumphed over a difficult childhood is often tempted to go to extremes with their own children in an attempt to create the perfect home and make life happy and carefree for their children.

My very good friend Victoria is the adult child of an alcoholic:

> My childhood was horrible. Life was turbulent and filled with violence. My dad almost killed my brother and me twice, repeatedly beat up my mom, shot a hole through the floor, and routinely raged uncontrollably, breaking things during his wild outbursts. I also remember my dad's explosive and sudden mood swings, causing us to fearfully walk "on egg shells." Of course, there was never any money. Naturally, no one was ever invited over to our home because you never knew what was going to happen. It all seems like a dreadful nightmare now.
>
> I constantly marvel at where God has brought me. I can't change the past. Being angry and resentful doesn't help anything. I want to bring up

my two boys to be men of character and confidence. Although I am thankful they will never experience anything similar to my life, I want to make certain that I don't go overboard making life too easy for them either.

In some respects, good parenting can be likened to keeping balance while carefully, cautiously treading a tightrope. It is easy to fall. It's tough to keep the intricate balance required. We want our children to enjoy happiness, the byproduct of character development, but we don't want to cripple them. We want to challenge our children, but not overly stress or discourage them. We want to encourage participation, but not force them or take away their confidence if they fail. We need balance. The stories shared by the children beg for balance. Children want their confidence built with encouragement and honesty, not with ridicule or dishonesty.

9

"My Child Is My First Priority"

"Confidence is believing in yourself and believing that
with God's help you can conquer any task."
—Sixth grader

The woman wanted a child but not a husband. She was a bright and accomplished professional and wanted an intelligent child. She investigated various options and became impregnated through a sperm bank.

The child was perfect in every way. Before too long, it became obvious that he was intellectually gifted and talented in the arts. He was also a handsome boy. The single mother was proud of her son, protective of him, and desired to create the best environment possible at home and at school.

Whenever he did not receive the highest grade or most prestigious honor possible, or when he was not deferred to by the other children, she made an appointment with the teacher or coach to find out what was going wrong. If she was not given the answer she wanted, she made an appointment with me.

The son was an appealing, likable child. He was well liked by his peer group, treated adults with respect, was responsible in his schoolwork, and worked to achieve his potential. In spite of the mother's predictable and ongoing interference, the boy was a favorite of everyone.

On this particular day, the mother was bugged about the awards given for the yearly science projects, which are displayed at Open House. Her child received a red ribbon, not the blue ribbon first prize. She wanted to make certain that the school understood that his project was the best. She presented her case with eloquence and passion. The teachers and I listened and responded with our reasoning, which she interpreted as "inadequate, fallacious, and prejudicial against my child."

I made several feeble attempts to convince the mother that her son could not always be expected to win or to be the best, nor was this desirable for his character development. The mother would not listen to such "foolishness." Then followed the words I shall never forget. "He has no father. I am all he has. That boy is my first priority. God is second. Nothing else counts." With that attitude, there was nothing left to say. The conference concluded with those words hanging in the air.

After thoroughly investigating other educational opportunities, the mother allowed the child to continue in our school. More frustration lay ahead for the singly focused woman. He son was not awarded the honor of being the valedictorian of the class. He did not earn the achievement. He tied with another for salutatorian, the second highest academic honor. It was a bitter blow for the mother. Because the boy is an idol the mother has created for all to join her in worshiping, the future holds increasingly severe disappointments.

Keep Priorities Straight

God never intended for parents to make idols of their children. When the mother said, "That boy is my first priority. God is second," she admitted to child worship. Her words and actions during the years in our school substantiated the fervor of her adoration and worship of her child. In contrast to her words and actions, God makes the priorities clear in the first three commandments: You may worship no other god than me. You shall not make yourselves any idols. You must never bow to an image or worship it in any way. In other words, you may not worship your children. You shall not make idols out of your children. You must never bow down to your children or worship them in any way. Such worship destroys the child's confidence as well as seriously affecting the parent.

A fifth grader expressed it succinctly this way, "Parents should not worship the child when they are trying to give confidence."

Shouldn't children be a top priority for parents? Absolutely! Above God? No. But shouldn't our children be a higher priority than our spouses? No. God first, then our spouses, and then our children. Children are definitely to be our third priority. If the husband or wife is not available due to death, divorce, or separation, then the children are the second priority, but never the first.

A friend of mine delivered her first child. Because of serious complications, there would be no more pregnancies. Before the mother left the hospital with her precious bundle, a caring nurse gave a word of advice. "I can tell how much you love this child, as well you should. As much as you love this child, do not ever let the child usurp the place of your husband in your affections or in your life." That was nearly twenty-five years ago. My friend never forgot that piece of wisdom and has shared it with many others through the years.

Parents love their children. Actually, I believe we parents give our lives for our children every day in so many ways. Of course they are a top priority for any conscientious parent. We sacrifice time, money, and energy for them. Very often we put our dreams on hold or give them up all together for the good of our children. I know I speak for most parents when I say that I would far rather have someone dislike me, reject me, or speak disparagingly of me than have my children endure such blows. So strong is our love for our children. "You can hate me, but please—love my children."

Unfortunately, I could relate story after story of spouses who discover, once the kids have left the home, that they have nothing else in common. Whatever common interests brought them together decades before have long since evaporated. They sit, looking at each other in restaurants, having nothing to share that does not involve the children. Sometimes the parents divorce, desiring to start a new life with a fresh set of goals and objectives. Other times, the couple is desperate for grandchildren who will renew their reason for living and give them something to talk about and a way to spend their time.

Finding the Balance

Keeping balance and perspective is a lifelong struggle in all areas, including parenting. How can a parent know when children are assuming the priority that God or the spouse is to have within the household? Answering these questions will provide clues.

→ Do your children know that your relationship with God is the most important relationship in your life?

→ Do your children comprehend that your relationship with your spouse is the second most important in your life?

→ Are your children routinely allowed to interrupt and control conversations that you and your spouse are trying to have?

➞ Do you and your spouse take time to be alone together on a regular basis?

➞ When you and your spouse are together, do you always talk about the children or do you have other areas of discussion and interest?

➞ Do you prefer being with your children to being with your spouse?

➞ Do you look forward to being alone with your spouse after your children are grown?

Many parents today have the additional responsibility of caring for their aging parents, often within the existing family household. This is a particularly difficult area, and your children need to be a part of the solution rather than being allowed to create an additional struggle for your time and attention. Children must learn to honor their grandparents and to put their own desires aside many times, just as they see you do. The small daily sacrifices that your children make for an aging grandparent are character-building opportunities and can strengthen the growing confidence of the children.

The brilliant English poet John Milton wrote a comment on confidence that provides an excellent confidence goal. "Confidence imparts a wondrous inspiration to its possessor. It bears him on in security, either to face danger unafraid or to endure trials without flinching." Now, read that statement with your child's name in place of *possessor* and *him*. Can you honestly say that your child is growing toward having the confidence that "bears him on in security," able to meet the inescapable dangers and trials of life with the assurance that confidence brings?

As you reflect on the nine myths that damage a

child's confidence, asking yourself the following questions will help you to focus on a specific plan for developing confidence in your children using the suggestions in this book while avoiding the pitfalls we have pointed out.

- What goals would you set for building the confidence of yourself and your children this year?

- What steps do you need to take?

- What gets in the way?

- What would you like to work on?

- What will you do this week?

- Over what areas of parenting do you want to assume more control?

- What areas do you need to let go of?

This little anonymous poem entitled "Confidence" captures a life perspective that conscientious parents would like to have be true of their children.

Confidence is speaking words of praise
In cheering other people's ways,
In doing just the best you can
With every task and every plan.
It's silence when your speech would hurt.
Politeness when your neighbor's curt.
It's deafness when the scandal flows,
And sympathy with others' woes.
It's courage when disaster falls.
It's patience when the hours are long.
It's found in laughter and in song.

It's in the silent time of prayer,
In times of joy and times of care.
In all of life with godly sense,
You walk and talk with confidence.

Endnotes

1. A child quoted in Pat Holt and Grace Ketterman, M.D., *When You Feel Like Screaming* (Wheaton, IL: Shaw, 1988) 24.

2. Quoted in "Wisdom to Live By," *Investor's Business Daily* 29 Dec. 1998.

3. Kelly Jackson, "Leaders and Success," *Investor's Business Daily* 21 Sept. 1998: A6.

4. Ibid.

5. Richard Carlson, Ph.D., *Don't Sweat the Small Stuff* (n.c.: Hyperion, 1997) 47.

6. Phillip Michaels, "Football Star Ricky Williams," *Investor's Business Daily,* 31 Dec. 1998: A4.

7. Charles Oliver, "Industrialist John D. Rockefeller," *Investor's Business Daily,* 26 Oct. 1998: A6.

8. Holt & Ketterman 70.

9. Eddie Carswell and Babbie Mason, "Trust His Heart," Mansen Music, 1989.

10. Carlson 193–94.

11. Amy Reynolds, "Tennis Champ Bjorn Borg," *Investor's Business Daily* 16 Dec. 1998: A5.

12. Dr. Laura Schlessinger and Rabbi Stewart Vogel, *The Ten Commandments* (New York: HarperCollins, 1998) 138.

13. Leigh Steinberg with Michael D'Orso, *Winning with Integrity* (n.c.: Villard Books, 1998) 26–27.

14. Schlessinger and Vogel 54.

15. Pat Holt and Grace Ketterman, M.D., *Don't Give In, Give Choices* (Wheaton, IL: Shaw, 1997) 19.